THE ART
OF
WORLDLY
WISDOM

A collection of aphorisms
from the work of
Baltasar Gracian

Translated by
Martin Fischer

BARNES
&NOBLE
B O O K S
NEW YORK

To the memory of
EDMUND MICHAEL BAEHR

This edition published by Barnes & Noble, Inc.

1993 Barnes & Noble Books

ISBN 0-56619-133-5 *gift edition*
ISBN 1-56619-530-6 *paperback*

Book design by Jim Sarfati

Printed and bound in the United States of America

MG 9 8 7 6 5 4
MP 9 8 7 6 5 4 3

THE ART
OF
WORLDLY
WISDOM

✥ Contents ✥

THE ART
♨ OF ♨
WORLDLY
WISDOM

E {} **1** {}
VERYTHING TODAY HAS its point, but the
art of making yourself count for something the greatest: more is demanded to produce one wise man today,
than seven formerly; and more is needed to deal with a
single individual in our times, than with a whole people in the past.

{} **2** {}

MIND AND SPIRIT. The two poles upon which
rests the firmament of our faculties: the one
without the other, a happiness by half: mind is not
enough, spirit is necessary. The lot of a fool, to fail in
his calling, professional, commercial, political, social.

❧ 3 ❧

MAINTAIN AN AIR of uncertainty about your business. Admiration for the new is what bestows value upon the accomplished. To play with cards exposed is neither useful, nor in good taste. Create anticipation by not declaring your purpose, and especially where the height of your office commands public attention display a bit of mystery about everything, and by it further the respect in which you are held: even when you show your hand escape the obvious; just as in the daily round you do not disclose your inner self to everyone. A prudent silence is the sacred vessel of wisdom. Purpose declared was never highly esteemed and commits itself to criticism in advance; and should it fail, the misfortune is doubled. Imitate, therefore, the ways of God in order to keep those about you watchful, and alert.

❧ 4 ❧

WISDOM, BACKED BY courage make great: because immortal, they immortalize: each is as great as his mind, and to him who knows, everything is possible. A man without knowledge, a world in darkness. Understanding, and will, they are the eyes and the hands; without courage the mind is dead.

७ॐ **5** ॐ९

CREATE DEPENDENTS. The idol is not created by the gilder, but by the genuflector; he who knows, desires more that man shall need him than thank him. To hold them expectant is the art of the courtier, to rely upon their thankfulness, the art of the peasant, for the first remembers as the second forgets. More is to be gained from dependence than from courtesy; he shortly turns his back upon the well who has drunk his fill, and the squeezed orange falls from a golden salver into the dung. When dependence goes, decent deportment goes, and with it respect. Let it be a lesson and the first from experience, to keep hope alive but never satisfied, remaining necessary always even to the crowned head; but do not carry this to the point of silence that he may commit error, or so far as to make incurable the mischief of another, for your personal profit.

७ॐ **6** ॐ९

A MAN AT his best. You are not so born: strive daily to develop yourself in your person, in your calling, until perfection is attained: the fullness of your every gift, of your every faculty. You will know it in the improvement of your taste, in the clarification of your thinking, in the maturity of your judgment, in the control of your will. Some never attain the perfect, something always being lacking, and others are late in coming to themselves. The man complete, wise in speech, wise in action, is admitted, yea, he is welcomed into that rare fellowship of those who understand.

৫৯ 7 ৯৭

AVOID OUTSHINING THE master. All victory is odious but victory over the master, either the part of stupidity, or of fate. Superiority has always been detested, and most thoroughly when greatest. A little care will serve to cloak your ordinary virtues; as you would hide your beauty, in careless dress. Some will deign to take place after you in matters of luck or of heart; but in intelligence, none, least of all a sovereign: for this is the sovereign attribute, wherefore any attack upon it is a crime against majesty. They are kings and they wish to be such in what is most kingly; they may abide being helped; but not surpassed, wherefore let advice given them appear more a jog to what they forgot, than a light to what they could not find. The stars in happy fashion teach us this lesson, for even though her children and bright, they are never so froward as to outshine the sun.

ᘏᕆ **8** ᕬᕽ

A MAN WITHOUT passion, the pledge of great loftiness of spirit which by its very superiority redeems a man from the yoke of vagrant and vulgar externals. There is no greater mastery than the mastery of self, and its passions, for it amounts to the triumph of free will; but even where passion overcomes the individual, it must not dare to touch his office, especially if it be a high one; this is the best way to spare yourself grief, and yet the shortest way to a good reputation.

ᘏᕆ **9** ᕬᕽ

B ELIE IN YOURSELF the weaknesses of your country. Water partakes of the qualities, good or bad, of the seams through which it flows; and man of the clime into which he is born. Some owe more to their country than others because a happier zenith lay above them. There is no nation, even of the most cultured, without some inborn defect which its neighbors will not at once strike upon, either for their caution, or their comfort. A commendable skill to eradicate such national weaknesses in yourself, or at least, to hide them: thus are you made unique among your kind, for what is least expected is most esteemed. There are weaknesses also of race, of rank, of profession, and of age, which if gathered together in one individual, and not curbed, yield an intolerable monster.

⊰ *10* ⊱

FORTUNE AND FAME: the one as fleeting as the other is lasting. The first for this life, the second for the next: the one against envy, the other against oblivion: good fortune is desired and may perhaps be wheedled, but fame must be won; the wish for fame is born of quality; Fama was and is the sister of the giants and she follows only the extraordinary, either the prodigies, or the monsters, that men acclaim, or hate.

⊰ *11* ⊱

LIVE WITH THOSE from whom you can learn; let friendly intercourse be a school for knowledge, and social contact, a school for culture; to make teachers of your friends is to join the need of learning to the joy of converse. Happiness among the understanding is mutual, rewarded for what they say by the approval they receive; and for what they hear, by what they learn; it is personal interest usually that draws men together but here it is glorified. A man of understanding seeks out the houses of those true noblemen which are more the stages of an heroic than the palaces of vanity. There exist men in this world, known to the discerning, who in their bearing are veritable exemplars of every greatness and whose train, even, constitutes a courtly academy of art and learning.

〰 **1 2** 〰

NATURE AND ART: the material and the workmanship. There is no beauty unaided, no excellence that does not sink to the barbarous, unless saved by art; it redeems the bad and perfects the good. Nature commonly forsakes us at her best; wherefore, take refuge in art. The best in nature is raw without art, and the excellent lacks half, if it lacks culture. Without cultivation every man is a clown and needs, no matter what his attributes, polish.

〰 **1 3** 〰

ACCOMPLISH YOUR ENDS, sometimes indirectly, and sometimes directly. Life is a struggle of man against man's malice, in which sagacity comes to grips with the strategy of design. It never does the indicated, yea, it takes aim to deceive; the fanfare is in the light but the execution is in the dark, the purpose being always to belie. Intention is revealed to divert the attention of the adversary, when it is changed to gain the end by what was unexpected. But insight has perspicacity, is wary, and waits behind its armor: sensing always the opposite of what it was to sense, and recognizing at once the real purpose of the trick; it allows every first hint to pass, lies in wait for a second, and even a third. The simulation of truth now mounts higher by glossing the deception and tries through truth itself to falsify: it changes the play in order to change the trick; and makes the real appear the phantom: founding the greatest fraud upon the greatest candor. But wariness is on watch seeing clearly what is intended, and covering the blackness that was clothed in light: recognizing that design most artful which looked most artless. In such fashion is the wiliness of Python matched against the whiteness of Apollo's penetrating rays.

❧ 14 ❧

THE SUBSTANCE, AND the form. The thing does not suffice, form as well is required. Bad form spoils everything, even justice and reason; while good form supplies everything, gilding the No, sweetening the truth, and perfuming decay itself: the how has much to do with things, and a little manner is the thief of the heart; good deportment is the gala dress of life, and in singular fashion the pledge of a happy ending to everything.

༔ *1 5* ༔

HAVE HELPFUL SPIRITS about you. The good
fortune of the mighty that they can surround
themselves with men of understanding who protect
them from the dangers of every ignorance, who disen-
gage them from the snarls of every difficulty. A singular
distinction, to be served by the wise; and better than
the barbarous taste of Tigranes, he who used captive
kings as servants. A new kind of lordship and of the
best in life: by art to make subjects of those whom
nature placed above you. Knowledge is long, and life is
short, and he who does not know, does not live.
Peculiarly smart, therefore, to learn without effort and
much from many, being taught by all. Later, in the
assembly this man speaks for the many, for through his
lips there speak all the sages that he drew upon for
counsel; thus does he gain the title of oracle through
the sweat of others. These superior souls first choose
the lesson: to teach it later as the quintessence of wisdom. Wherefore let him who cannot manage to have
wisdom in his train, at least strive to be familiar with it.

༔ *1 6* ༔

KNOWLEDGE WITH GOOD intent. They
assure the happy issue of every undertaking.
Good endowment joined to bad purpose has always

yielded a monster. Evil intent is the venom in every capacity and, supported by knowledge, a poison more subtile; an unholy sovereignty, that which devotes itself to destruction! Science without conscience, compounded madness!

❧ 1 7 ❧

CHANGE YOUR STYLE; not always in the same fashion, in order to divert the attention, and especially if you are being rivalled. Not always directly, or they will know your course, anticipate you, and frustrate even your intent. It is easy to kill the bird on the wing that flies straight; not that which turns. Nor always indirectly, for that trick is learned after the second feint. Malice is ever alert and much thought is necessary to outwit her; a gambler does not play the card which his opponent expects much less that which he desires.

❧ 1 8 ❧

INDUSTRY AND MINERVA. Without both, no distinction, and with both, this in the highest degree. Mediocrity gets further with industry, than superiority without it. Reputation is bought for the price of labor, and what has cost little is worth little. To attain even the highest posts, many have lacked only industry; rarely has their talent been insufficient. To prefer to be a second in a high position to being a first in a low has good excuse; but to be satisfied with being a second in the lowest, when able to be a first, has none. Well, talent and art are both called for, but industry sets the seal.

᷾᷾ *1* **9** ᷾᷾

DO NOT ENTER where too much is anticipated. It is the misfortune of the over celebrated, that they cannot measure up to the excessive expectations of them afterwards: never can the actual attain the imagined: for to think perfection is easy, but to incarnate it, most difficult; the imagination weds the wish and together they always conjure up more than reality can furnish. For however great may be a man's excellencies, they will not suffice to satisfy what was imagined of him, and when men see themselves cheated in their extravagant anticipations, they turn more quickly to disparagement than to praise. Hope is a great falsifier of the truth; let the intelligence put her right by seeing to it that the fruit is superior to the appetite: sound principle of faith, to excite anticipation without endangering the object of your appearance: a better exit, when the actual transcends the imagined, and is more than was expected. But this rule fails in the case of evil men, for exaggeration overbuilds them too, so that when this picture is joyously reduced, what was feared as a monster of villainy comes to appear as something quite normal.

૨૬ **2 0** ૐ૬

A MAN OF your century. Great men are a part of their times. Not all were born into a period worthy of them, and many so born failed to benefit by it: some merited a better century, for all that is good does not always triumph: fashions have their periods and even the greatest virtues, their styles: but the philosopher has one advantage, he is ageless; and should this not prove his century, many to follow, will.

૨૬ **2 1** ૐ૬

THE ART OF being lucky. There are rules to luck, for to the wise not all is accident; try, therefore, to help luck along. Some are satisfied to stand politely before the portals of Fortuna and to await her bidding; better those who push forward, and who employ their enterprise, who on the wings of their worth and valor seek to embrace luck and effectively to gain her favor. And yet, properly reasoned, there is no other way to her but that of virtue and attentiveness: for none has more good luck, or more bad luck, than he has wisdom, or unwisdom.

ॐ **2 2** ॐ

A MAN WELL-INFORMED. The bastions of men of the world are a gentlemanly and distinguished learning: a broad understanding of all that is going on, but in uncommon fashion, not common; they have wit and wisdom on their tongues and they know how to use either on proper occasion: for more is often accomplished through a witty remark than through the gravest argument. And common sense has availed many a man more than the seven arts, however liberal they may be.

ॐ **2 3** ॐ

TO BE FLAWLESS. The requisite of perfection, yet few live without some weaknesses, either of the spirit or of the flesh, and they are tormented by them when they could so easily overcome them. The critical judgment of another is always offended when some slight defect defaces a heavenly set of gifts, for a single cloud is enough to obscure the whole of a sun. Such are the shadows upon a reputation, which malice is ever quick to discover but as slow to forget. The greatest of achievements would be to transform these flaws into adornments. By such trick did Caesar know how to cover his in-born ugliness with laurel.

❧ 2 4 ☙

HARNESS THE IMAGINATION: sometimes curbing her, sometimes giving her rein, for she is the whole of happiness, and sets to rights even the understanding: she sinks to tyranny, not satisfied with mere faith, but demanding works, thus becoming the mistress of life itself, which she does with pleasure or with pain, according to the nonsense presented; for she makes men contented or discontented with themselves: dangling before some, noting but the spectre of their eternal suffering, thus becoming the scourge of these fools: and showing to others nothing but fortune and romance, while merrily laughing. Of all this is she capable if not held in check by the wisest of wills.

❧ 2 5 ☙

OF SOUND UNDERSTANDING. The art of arts, once, to meditate; but this no longer suffices, for today one must be able to divine, in order to escape being deceived: he cannot be understanding who does not understand. There are diviners of the heart, and lynxes of the intent; the truths for which most we thirst, are but half uttered, and only the observant gets them all: in everything that you would hear, hold a tight rein on your credulity, in everything you would not hear, use the spur.

❧ **2 6** ❧

DISCOVER EACH MAN'S thumbscrew. It is the way to move his will, more skill than force being required to know how to get at the heart of anyone: there is no will without its leanings, which differ as desires differ. All men are idolaters, some of honor, others of greed, and the most of pleasure: the trick lies in knowing these idols that are so powerful, thus knowing the impulse that moves every man: it is like having the key to another man's will, with which to get at the spring within, by no means always his best, but more frequently his worst, for there are more unholy men in this world than holy: divine the ruling passion of a man, excite him with a word, and then attack him through his pet weakness, that invariably checkmates his free will.

❧ **2 7** ❧

RATE THE INTENSIVE above the extensive. The perfect does not lie in quantity, but in quality. All that is best is always scant, and rare, for mass in anything cheapens it. Even among men the giants have often been true pygmies. Some judge books by their thickness, as though they had been written to exercise the arms, instead of the mind. Bigness, alone, never gets beyond the mediocre, and it is the curse of the universal man, that in trying to be everything, he is nothing. It is quality that bestows distinction, and in heroic proportions if the substance is sublime.

?֍ **2 8** ֍?

IN NOTHING VULGAR. Not in taste. Oh, how wise! he who was cast down because his efforts found favor with the many: the hosannas of the mulitude can never bring satisfaction to the discerning. Yet there exist those chameleons of popularity, who find their joy, not in the sweet breath of Apollo, but in the smell of the crowd. And not in mind: not taken in by what are miracles to the populace, for the ignorant do not rise above marvelling. Thus the stupidity of a crowd is lost in admiration, even as the brains of an individual uncovers the trick.

?֍ **2 9** ֍?

A JUST MAN. He stands on the side of the right with such conviction, that neither the passion of a mob, nor the violence of a despot can make him overstep the bounds of reason. But who will be this Phoenix of impartiality? For justice knows few so completely dedicated to her. Many praise her, but not for themselves: others follow her until danger threatens: and then the false deny her, and the political betray her: for she pays no heed in her dealings to friendship, to power, or even to personal profit, and herein lies the danger of her disavowal: with plausible metaphysics the sly now forsake her, for they would not offend, either their higher reason, or the state: but a man true to himself deems such dissimulation a species of treason, esteeming staunchness above cleverness, finding himself wherever the truth is found, and if he changes his loyalties, it is not because of fickleness in him, but because they first changed on him.

৯ঌ 3 0 ঌ৯

TAKE NO PART in foolish enterprises; much less in schemes more likely to injure, than to enhance your reputation. There exist all kinds of questionable cliques, and a thinking man flees the lot. As well as those men of strange taste who forever marry what wiser men have divorced: they live well paid for their singularity: and even if they attract notice, it is more by the derision they evoke than the commendation. Wherefore the circumspect will not allow himself to be made conspicuous even in his profession: much less, ridiculous in those matters that concern his person: they need not be listed, for general disapprobation has sufficiently labelled them.

ఇస 3 1 ఇస

KNOW THE LUCKY, in order to hold to them, and the unlucky, in order to flee from them. Hard luck is mostly the punishment of foolishness, and no disease is so catching for the mourners: never open the door to a small misfortune, for many more always creep in behind it, and greater ones, under its protection. The great trick in cards lies in knowing what to discard: and the deuce of a suit that is trump, is more valuable than the ace of a suit that was. When in doubt, there is safety in sticking with the intelligent and the prudent, for, sooner or later, they catch up with luck.

ఇస 3 2 ఇస

BE GRACIOUS: for those who govern it is the grand manner through which to please: it is the halo of the mighty by which they gain the good will of a populace. This is the single advantage of power, that it enables the holder to do more good: those are friends who make friends. There are those, on the other hand, who can never be gracious, not so much because of peevishness, as of meanness, the very opposite in everything of the divine virtue.

❧ 3 3 ❧

K NOW HOW TO draw away, for if it is a great rule of life to know how to refuse, it becomes an even greater to know how to refuse yourself; either to business or to persons: there are extraneous occupations, which are the very moths of precious time: and it is worse to be busy about the trivial, than to do nothing; it is not enough for the observant that he does not obtrude; a greater need to see to it that others do not obtrude upon him. Do not belong so wholly to others, that you no longer belong to yourself, even though you may not exploit your friends, nor ask of them more than they care to give: for everything carried to excess becomes a vice, and especially in matters of the daily round: an intelligent moderateness best holds the good will, and the respect, for it does not bruise the so precious proprieties: maintain therefore the freedom of your being, worship the beautiful; and do not give offence to the laws of your own good taste.

❧ 3 4 ❧

K NOW YOUR CHIEF asset, your great talent, cultivate it, and help along the others. Anyone might have attained eminence in something, had he but known his advantage; discover therefore your regal attribute; and freight it to the full: some excel in judgment, others in courage. Most men violate their Minerva, and thus rise to the heights in nothing: for what is too quick in satisfying the passion, is too late in pointing out its error.

❧ 3 5 ☙

THINK, AND MOST about that which is most important: all the fools get lost because they do not think: they never see the half of things, and knowing neither their loss, nor their profit, they make small effort in either direction. Some make much of what is of little importance, or little of what is of much importance, always judging wrong. Most do not lose their heads because they have none. There are matters which should be considered with every faculty, and then be treasured in the depths of the mind. An intelligent man thinks about everything, though with discrimination, digging deepest where there are prospect, and treasure; knowing always that more lies buried than he knows; by such means does what is apprehended become what is comprehended.

❧ 3 6 ☙

KNOW THE MEASURE of your luck: either to play upon it, or to get out from under it; more important, far, than to note the weather, for if he is a fool who before forty has not turned to Hippocrates for health; what greater fool, he who by this time has not turned to Seneca for wisdom. It takes great skill to manage luck, at times through patience, since there is merit in patience, at times through push, for luck has moments and moods: even though they are hard to recognize, so irregular is her course. Let him who finds her propitious, strike, for luck loves the bold; as gallantry loves the young. But let him who meets her otherwise do nothing, let him retire: lest to the bad luck prevailing there be invited more from afar.

༃ 3 7 ༄

KNOW WHAT WIMBLING is. For it is a fine point in human intercourse. It is done to test the spirit, and by it one may with unconcern probe the most hidden, and the deepest recesses of the heart. Sometimes it is malicious, sharp, poisoned with the juice of envy, and dipped in the venom of passion, unnoticed darts aimed to bring down the sublime, and the estimable. Many have fallen from the favor of high or low, wounded by some trifling word: who earlier never feared a whole conspiracy of popular hatred and personal spleen. At other times it works differently, through flattery aiding and abetting, the self-esteem. But with the same skill with which a plot is projected, let caution recognize it, and attentiveness expect it: for defence depends upon recognition, and the shot foreseen always fails its mark.

༠ぁ **3 8** ぁ

SAY FAREWELL TO luck when winning: it is the way of the gamblers of reputation: quite as important as a gallant advance is a well-planned retreat, wherefore lock up your winnings when they are enough, or when great. Continuous luck is always suspect; more secure is that which changes, and which, half bitter and half sweet, is more satisfying even to the taste: the more luck pyramids, the greater the danger of slip, and of collapse: for luck always compensates her intensity by her brevity. Fortune wearies of carrying anyone long upon her shoulders.

༠ぁ **3 9** ぁ

RECOGNIZE THINGS WHEN at their best, in their season, and know how to enjoy them then. The works of nature all mount to a peak of perfection; up to it they wax, beyond it they wane. Only in matters of art have a few gone to the point where they might not be improved. It is the mark of cultivated taste to enjoy everything at its best: but all may not do this, and not all who may, know how. Even the fruits of the spirit have their moment of ripeness, and it is well to recognize this, in order to value it properly and to minister to it.

ᖋ **4 0** ᖋ

THE GOOD WILL of men. To gain the popular admiration is much; but to gain its affection, more; something depends upon the stars, but more upon effort, for while the former give birth, the latter brings development; great gifts are not enough, even when they exist, but he easily finds the way, who has found the will. Wherefore good deeds are required to engender good will: do good and with both hands; be generous in speech and more generous in deed, love in order to be loved, for true nobleness is the politic magic of the great. Turn the hand first to achievement, and then to the pen, from the blade of the sword to the blade of history, for there is such a thing as the blessing of the biographers, for it makes immortal.

ᖋ **4 1** ᖋ

NEVER EXAGGERATE: a matter of great importance, to forego superlatives, in part to avoid offending the truth, in part to avoid the cheapening of your judgment. Exaggeration wastes distinction, and testifies to the paucity of your understanding, and your taste. Praise excites anticipation, and stimulates desire, and afterwards when value does not measure up to price, disappointment turns against the fraud and takes revenge by cheapening both the appraised and the appraiser. For this reason let the prudent go slowly, and err in understatement rather than overstatement. The extraordinary of every kind is always rare, wherefore temper your estimate. Exaggeration is akin to lying; and through it you jeopardize your reputation for good taste, which is much, and for good judgment, which is more.

ॐ **4 2** ॐ

A RULER BORN. It is the hidden strength of superiority: never the issue of a pomposity, but that of a natural imperiousness. All become subject to it without knowing why, recognizing in it the hidden power of born authority. These sovereign spirits are kings by merit, and lions by innate right, who capture the hearts, and even the minds of all about them, through the faith they inspire: when blessed with other gifts, they are born to be the prime movers of mankind, for they can accomplish more with one word, than others with a thousand.

ॐ **4 3** ॐ

THINK AS THE few, and speak as the many. To swim against the current is just as useless for setting a matter right, as it is dangerous for the swimmer. Only a Socrates may try it: to disagree with another is deemed an insult, for it is a condemnation of his judgment: the offended soon multiply, at times because their cause, at times because their champion has been hurt; the truth is for the few, the false is for the populace, because popular. A wise man cannot be recognized by what he says in the public square, for there he does not speak with his tongue, but with that of the general foolishness, the more so as by this means he better disguises his inner self: just so does the prudent not expose himself to contradiction, as he does not contradict; quick as he may be in judgment, so slow is he in making it public. Thinking is free, and it may not be, nor can it be strangled; let the wise man take refuge in his silence, and when at times he permits himself to speak, let it be in the shelter of the few, and the understanding.

ঔ 4 ঙ

A SYMPATHY WITH great men. It is the talent of the great to agree with the great: a veritable wonder of nature both because of its mystery, and because of its usefulness. It makes kindred the hearts, and the minds of men: and its effects are such as the common ignorance attributes to love potions. It not only leads to better mutual respect, but advances good will, even inclining men to each other; it convinces without argument, and gets things done without effort. It may be active, or it may be passive, but either, a happiness sublime: a great art, to recognize, to value, and to know how to attain it, for no amount of doggedness suffices without this hidden gift.

ఇ 45 ఇ

BE SHREWD, BUT not too shrewd. Something not to be assumed, much less exposed: all artfulness must be concealed for it is suspect, especially that of forsightedness, which is hated. Deceit fills the world, wherefore be doubly suspicious: but without letting it be seen, for that would destroy trust in you; suspicion vexes the spirit, and cries for revenge, awakening evils of which no one dreamed. To have considered well how to proceed, is of great advantage for the day's work: and there is no better evidence of a man's good sense. The perfection of an undertaking lies in the masterly sureness with which it was executed.

ఇ 46 ఇ

TEMPER YOUR ANTIPATHIES. We seem to hate with pleasure, and even before we have looked; and always does this inborn and vulgar aversion rise against the most eminent of men. Let the intelligence overcome it, because nothing can more cheapen us, than that we hate our betters: for as a sympathy with the great enhances our standing, antipathy to them only lowers our own.

❧ 47 ❧

AVOID AFFAIRS OF honor. It is the first business of prudence. Men of great capacity are not easily taxed to their limits: it takes much to drive them to one side or the other, for they always keep to the middle course of their common sense, being slow to come to a rupture, for it is much easier to get into something than to get out of something, well. These affairs are the tempters of good sense, and it is safer to flee from them, than to win through them. One matter of honor drags in another and a worse, and things are then close to the edge of downfall. There are men who by nature, or even by nationality, are easily excited: they find it easy to involve themselves in obligations of this sort: but he who walks by the light of reason, always considers carefully. He will deem it better courage not to become ensnarled, than to win, and even should the everpresent fool bob up, he will excuse himself on the ground that he does not wish to be another.

❧ 48 ❧

A MAN OF substance, for in such measure does he count as something. There ought always to be much more on the inside, than on the outside of everything. Some men are all front, like houses half-finished for lack of funds, having the entrances of a palace, but the contents of a hut: there is nothing in them for which to stop, or to be stopped by, because the first greetings over, converse also is over. They enter to make their bows, like Sicilian horses, but presently go silent, for words soon fail to flow where there is no spring of thought. They take in easily those who are equally superficial; but not the intelligent, for as these look deeper and find nothing, the fiction is recognized by the discerning.

৵ৡ **4 9** ৵ৡ

A MAN OF insight, and of judgment. He commands the world, and the world does not command him. He plumbs at once the greatest depth; and he knows how to get at the anatomy of a soul to perfection. For him to look at a man is to see through him, and to understand him to the core. Through uncommon observation, he becomes the great decipherer of that which is most deeply hidden. He looks sharply, sees clearly, and deduces rightly; all that he uncovers, he takes in, he grasps, he comprehends.

৵ৡ **5 0** ৵ৡ

D O NOTHING TO make you lose respect for yourself, or to cheapen yourself in your own eyes: let your own integrity be the standard of rectitude, and let your own dictates be stricter than the precepts of any law. Forego the unseemly, more because of this fear of yourself, than for fear of the sternness of outer authority: learn this fear of yourself; and there will then be no need for that imaginary monitor of Seneca.

?ॐ **5 1** ॐ

A MAN OF DISCERNMENT. The most of life is that; it calls for good taste, and the best of judgment, for neither learning nor mind is enough. There is nothing perfect where there is not choice: two qualities are required, the power to choose, and the power to choose the better. And yet in this, many of fertile mind, and subtle, of sharp understanding, of learning and experience, always fail: forever consorting with the worse, as though determined to go wrong, wherefore this comes to be one of the greatest gifts from on high.

?ॐ **5 2** ॐ

N EVER LOSE YOUR head, a matter of great practical wisdom, never to let it get away from you: it marks the great man, and of noble heart, for all greatness is hard to throw off balance. The passions are the humors of the spirit, and their every excess makes sick the mind; and if the disease escapes through the mouth, it endangers the reputation. Wherefore have such mastery over self, and be so strong, that nothing,

either in the greatest fortune or in the greatest adversity, can upset you, remaining superior even to the admiration of this feat.

∂ᰥ **5 3** ᰥ∾

ILIGENT, AND INTELLIGENT. Diligence
quickly accomplishes what the intelligence has
well thought out. Haste is the passion of fools, and as
they know not the difficulties, they work without
heed: wiser men, on the other hand, are likely to fail
from overcaution; for of reflection is bred delay: and so
their hesitation in acting loses them the fruits of their
good judgment. Promptitude is the mother of fortune.
He does much who leaves nothing for tomorrow. A
magnificent motto: to make haste slowly.

∂ᰥ **5 4** ᰥ∾

AVE STRENGTH OF spirit. It is out of a dead
lion that even the rabbits pull the hairs, for there
is no sneering at courage; if concession is made in one
instance, it will have to be made in a second, and so on
even to the last: and the same effort required to win
late, would have availed more if expended earlier.
Courage of the spirit is more than courage of the body:
it is like a sword sheathed in the scabbard of your
heart, and ready for the occasion. It is the protector of
your person: but more against the hurt of its soul than

the hurt of its flesh. Many have been rich in mind, but because they were poor in this courage of the spirit, they lived as the dead, and died for what they lacked, for it is not without plan that nature has joined the sweetness of the honey with the sharpness of the sting in the bee; nerves and bones make up the body, let not its spirit be all softness.

෯ 5 5 ෨

A MAN WHO can wait, for it marks a great heart endowed with patience; never to be in undue haste, or excited. Be first the master of yourself, and you will thereafter be the master of others; one must journey far through time to get to the core of anything. A prudent waiting brings season to accomplishment and ripeness to what is hidden. The crutch of time accomplishes more than the iron club of Hercules. God himself does not tame with a whip, but with time: a great truth this: Time, and I 'gainst any two. Fortune herself crowns patience with the heaviest of garlands.

෯ 5 6 ෨

HAVE GOOD IMPULSES: they are the fruit of a happy swiftness of the spirit: fearing neither hazard nor accident, because of their faith in their own vitality: and their alertness: some think long only to go wrong in everything afterwards; and others succeed in everything without ever having thought before. They are veritable machines which function best when under strain; they are freaks who when pushed, succeed at everything but, given time, at nothing; what does not come to them at once never comes, for there is nothing to which they may appeal afterwards. The quick are always well received, because their very appearance argues capacity, of their minds by their alertness, and of their labors, by their spirit.

᎒Ꮚ **5 7** ᎒Ꮚ

THAT DONE WITH deliberation is done quickly enough, and better: what is made in haste is unmade as soon; and what is to last an eternity, may well tarry another in its creation: nothing arrests the attention unless it be perfect, and perfection alone makes accomplishment eternal. The mind that has profundity attains immortality, that being worth most, which has cost most, for even the most precious of the metals is that which is slowest to melt, and the heaviest.

᎒Ꮚ **5 8** ᎒Ꮚ

KNOW HOW TO change your front: do not show yourself in like fashion to everybody; and do not expend more energy than a business warrants; waste nothing, either of knowledge, or of strength: a good falconer does not loose more birds than suffice to get the game: do not put everything into the showcase at once, or none will pause to admire on another day. Always keep something new in reserve with which to dazzle to-morrow, for he who thus uncovers something fresh each day, maintains the interest, and never allows the limits of his treasury to be discovered.

?ह **5 9** ஜ

MAKE A GOOD exit. He who enters the house of fortune through the gate of pleasure, leaves it through the gate of sorrow; and conversely: keep in mind therefore the curtain, paying greater heed to the happy exit, than to the applauded entrance. It is the fate of the unlucky to be off to a happy start, and to a most tragic finish: there is no point to the applause of the vulgar on appearance, for everybody gets it; but there is, to the feeling which remains on exit, for those encored are rare, and fortune follows few as they leave; polite as she is to the arriving, equally discourteous is she to the departing.

?ह **6 0** ஜ

JUST IN JUDGMENT. Some men are born wise: with an inborn sense of right and wrong they enter upon a prudent conduct of life, and thus half their journey to success is over: the years, and experience, develop their understanding, and so they attain a judgment

most tempered: they despise all prejudice as a tempta-
tion of the spirit, especially in matters of state, which,
because of their great importance, demand absolute
uprightness. They deserve to have direction of the ship
of state, either to steer it, or to lay its course.

ৰ্ভ **6 1** ৰ্ভ

PREEMINENCE IN WHAT is best. The special in
the general of the perfections. No chance to be the
hero if not possessed of some sublime attribute.
Mediocrities are not the subjects of applause. Only
eminence in a high calling cuts a man out of the common herd to place him in the class of the rare. To be
excellent in a humble calling is to be something, but in
something small: it may carry much of what brings
delight but only little of what brings fame. To be excellent in great things, is to assume the character of a sovereign, it evokes admiration, and it gains good will.

ৰ্ভ **6 2** ৰ্ভ

WORK WITH GOOD tools. Some seek to
exhibit their cleverness by pointing to the poor
qualities of their tools: a dangerous type of self-satisfaction to be followed by stiff punishment. The excellence of a servant has never dulled the splendor of the
master: for all the glory of what is accomplished later
descends upon the first cause, as, in reverse, all the dis-

grace. Fame walks only with principals; she never says: this one had a good subordinate and that one, a bad; but only: this one did well, and that one did poorly. Hence, choose well, make study, for thereon depends the immortality of your reputation.

ৡ৾ **6 3** ঙ

XCELLENT, TO BE first in any line, and doubly excellent if the line is great; a big advantage to be the player of the hand, if the deal has been fair. Many a man might have been a Phoenix at his job had there not been others before him: the first in any line are crowned primogenitures by fame, and the rest must beg their bread for however much they sweat, they cannot rid themselves of the vulgar charge of imitation. The mark of the extraordinary to have blazed new trails to glory; and in such fashion, that the intelligence assured the success of the enterprise from the start. By the mere business of being the first in any undertaking shrewd men have made a place for themselves in the roster of the heroic. For which reason some men have preferred to be firsts in a second class, to being seconds in a first.

ৡ৾ **6 4** ঙ

NOW HOW TO escape grief, a profitable maxim, for it is the way to escape regret. A little prudence helps much, for she is the light of happiness, and therefore of peace. Be not the purveyor of scandal, or yet its recipient, but forbid it entrance, much less give it aid. One man keeps his ears only to have them bathed in sweet flattery; another, only to have them deafened by the bitterness of evil gossip; for there are those who cannot live without some daily dirt, as Mirthridates could not, without his poison. Neither is it the law of self-preservation, that you must wish upon yourself a lifelong regret, in order to provide momentary pleasure to another, however close to you: never sin against your own happiness, in order to comfort another, who comes for advice, and then does not stay: for in every situation, which spells joy to another and pain to you, this is the proper rule; it is better that he be downcast today, than that you be tomorrow, and helpless in the matter to boot.

৯৯ **6 5** ৯৯

O F CULTIVATED TASTE. It can be cultivated even as the intelligence: the better the appreciation, the greater the appetite, and when fulfilled, the greater the enjoyment. Greatness of spirit is known by the richness of the things needed to gratify it: for it takes much to satisfy a great capacity: just as much food is required for large hunger: even so does the sublime in spirit demand the sublime in matter. The boldest objects of nature fear this judgment of taste; and the finest in art trembles before it: few are the stars of the first magnitude, let appreciation of them be equally choice. Taste and contact have a way of going together, and the inheritance is in line: wherefore he is fortunate who may consort with those who have taste at its best. But neither should a trade be made of dissatisfaction with everything, for that is the extreme of fools, and odious in proportion to its affectation, and its intemperateness. Some would wish God to create another world, and of wholly different ideals, in order to satisfy their crazy phantasies.

≈§ **6 6** §≈

KEEP IN MIND the happy ending. Many lay greater stress upon the rules in the way to an end than upon the happy attainment of that end: and yet the shame of failure has always outweighed any approbation of the pains taken in accomplishments. He who wins, does not have to explain. Most men see nothing of the means to an end, but only the good or the bad issue thereof: and so none endangers his reputation, who accomplishes his end. A happy finish gilds everything, however unfitting the means may have been. Which explains why at times it should be the rule to offend the rules, when it is not possible by other methods to attain a happy ending.

ᚾ 6 7 ᚾ

CHOOSE AN OCCUPATION that brings distinction. Most things depend upon the satisfaction they give others: and appreciation is to talent what the west wind is to the flowers, breath, and life itself. There are occupations which enjoy public acclaim; and there are others, even though more important, which receive no recognition: the former because done in the sight of everybody win popular favor: the latter, even though they possess more of the rare and the worthy, remain unnoticed, because done in obscurity; they may be venerated, but they receive no approbation. Among princes, it is the victorious who are celebrated; and it is for this reason that the kings of Aragon are so highly honored, as warriors, conquerors, and great men. Let the man of gifts find himself a place thus prized, where all may see him, and all may play a part with him, for then will the voice of the people hold him immortal.

ᚾ 6 8 ᚾ

TO JOG THE understanding is a greater feat, than to jog the memory: for it takes more to make a man think, than to make him remember. Some fail to strike, when the iron is hot, because they fail to see the opportunity, wherefore let a bit of friendly advice help them to see their chance. One of the great attributes of the mind is its power to know when opportunity offers:

but where such mind is lacking, many things fail to be done which might have been: on which account let him give light who has it, and let him seek it who needs to, the former with reserve, the latter, with ardor: but let it not be more than mere suggestion; such reticence is necessary, and in proportion to the stake involved of him who makes it: show your interest, and go beyond it but not too far: if you receive a No, go in search of a Yes, but with art, for in most instances nothing is won, because nothing was ventured.

ॐ *6 9* ॐ

NOT THE SLAVE of vulgar moods. A great man, he who is never the victim of passing fancies. A good precept, to meditate upon yourself; to discover your present mood, and to prepare against it: or even to throw yourself into an opposite one, in order to come to rest, between the natural and the assumed, on the balance point of common sense: it is a first principle that in order to improve yourself, you must first know yourself, for there exist veritable monsters of moodiness, always of a different temper, and of a different mind with each; eternally enslaved by their smug intemperance, they involve themselves most consistently, their excess checkmating not only their purpose, but attacking their judgment, thus defeating both their ends and their plan.

❧ 7 0 ❧

K NOW HOW TO refuse. Since you cannot accede to everything, or to everybody, it becomes important to know how not to accede; and especially in those who command; for here enters manner. The No of one man is more esteemed, than the Yes of another; for a No that is gilded may be more satisfying than a Yes unembellished. There are many who carry an eternal No in the mouth with which they spoil everything. It always comes first, so that even when later they grant everything, such answer gives little satisfaction, because of the bad taste provided by the first. Refusal should never be flat, the truth appearing by degrees, nor should it be absolute, for that would cancel dependence, wherefore some remnant of hope must be kept alive, to sweeten the bitterness of the refusal. Employ courtliness to fill the void of the denial, and let pleasing words disguise the failure of action. Yes and No are quickly spoken, but they demand long consideration.

❧ 7 1 ❧

N OT ECCENTRIC: not freakish in manner, either by nature or by affectation. A thinking man is ever the same in all he does, for upon this is founded his reputation as a man of wisdom: change in him depends upon himself and has its causes, and its reasons;

in matters of common sense mere moodiness is something abhorrent. There are those who are of different face daily, until even their judgment goes awry, in like proportion their will, and so even, their luck: what was their luck: what was yesterday the white of their Yes, is today the black of their No: always ruining the good opinion, and be fogging the concept men had of them.

ఇక 7 2 కిక

A MAN OF DECISION: less censurable is poor execution, than irresolution; for matter in flux does not putrefy as does matter stagnant. Some men are so incapable of decision that they need constantly to be prodded from without; and this springs at times less from a confused judgment, since theirs may be unusually clear, than from unwillingness to act. An evidence of genius to foresee difficulties; but an evidence of greater genius to be able to see the way out of such difficulties. Others are embarrassed by nothing, and possessed as they are of great judgment and determination, they are born for the highest posts, because their quick comprehension eases the day's business, and speeds it: whatever they tackle is soon finished, so that after having set one world in order, time is left to start upon another: and inasmuch as they feel that luck is with them, they fare forth in all confidence.

ॐ 73 ॐ

KNOW THE MEANING of evasion. It is the prudent man's way of keeping out of trouble; with the gallantry of a witty remark he is able to extricate himself from the most intricate of labyrinths. He emerges gracefully from the bitterest encounter and with a smile. It was to this that the greatest of the great captains ascribed his power. A courteous way of saying No, is to change the conversation, nor is there greater politeness than that of not being able to understand.

ॐ 74 ॐ

NOT UNAPPROACHABLE. It is in the government that the really ungoverned have their being; to be unapproachable is the vice of men who do not know themselves, in that they confuse their spleen with their splendor: the road to affection does not lie in surliness. A show indeed, one of these erratics, making a point of his exclusiveness! His unfortunate subordinates, enter to have speech, as to battle with a tiger; as full of spears, as of fears. To win office, such a man could get himself in with everybody, but having arrived, his presumptuousness gets him out with everybody. Because of his place he should be accessible to the many, but because of his gall, or his spite, he becomes accessible to none. A just punishment, to let him be, thus robbing him both of his brains and his following.

ᲒᎦ **7 5** ᎠᏕ

CHOOSE A HEROIC ideal, more as something to emulate, than as something to imitate. Examples of greatness lie about us, living texts of renown: let each set before himself the greatest in his line, not so much as something to follow, as something to spur him on. Alexander did not weep over Achilles dead, but over himself unborn, as yet, to glory. There is nothing that so thrills the ambition, as the clarion of another's fame. For that same impulse which buries jealousy, lifts up the noble spirit.

ᲒᎦ **7 6** ᎠᏕ

NOT THE JESTER always; the common sense of a man is found in his seriousness, for wisdom ranks higher than wit. He who is always the buffoon, is really never the man. He classes himself with the liar, in that neither is believed; not the latter, because his word is doubted; and not the former, because of his scoffing. For it is never known if what was said was weighed in the mind, which in no instance can have been much. There is nothing more banal than continuous banter. Thus some get the reputation of being witty, but they endanger thereby their reputation of being wise. The humorous may be allowed its moment, but for all the rest, the serious.

⅋ 7 7 ⅋

KNOW HOW TO be all things to all men. A wise Proteus, he who is learned with the learned, and with the pious, pious: it is the great way of winning all to you: for to be like, is to be liked. Observe each man's spirit and adapt yourself: to the serious, or to the jovial, as the case may be, by following the fashion, through a politic change within yourself: a veritable necessity in those who are dependent. But this great rule of life calls for rich talent: being least difficult to that man of the world whose mind is filled with knowledge, and whose spirit is filled with taste.

⅋ 7 8 ⅋

ART IN EXECUTION. Fools always rush in, for all fools are rash. Their very simplicity, which at the start makes them insensible to advice, at the finish makes them insensible to disgrace. But the wise enter with great care; their bodyguards are watchfulness, and caution: these scout out the hidden, so that progress may be made without danger: for to dash in regardless stands condemned by discretion as foolhardy, even though luck at times absolves the venturer. Go slowly where the shoals are many. Let foresight feel the way, and let caution determine the ground: there are today great shallows in the human sea, so proceed always with the leadline.

ᜒᜓ **7 9** ᜒᜓ

O F HAPPY MIND. In moderation, it is an asset, and not a liability. A bit of humor seasons everything. The greatest man plays the fool at times, for it makes him popular; only his manners are forever checked by his mind, and proper homage is paid to decorum. Some can make of a bit of wit a short cut out of every difficulty, for certain things should be taken lightly and often the very ones which others take most seriously. He who shows himself affable, captures all hearts.

ᜒᜓ **8 0** ᜒᜓ

A LERT WHEN SEEKING information. We live for the most part by what is told us; it is little that we see: thus we live in the faith of others; the ear is the side door of truth, but the front door of falsehood. The truth is sometimes seen, but rarely heard: on the fewest of occasions does it arrive in its elemental purity, especially if it has travelled far, for then it is always soiled by what has happened on the road: for feeling tinges with her colors all that she touches, sometimes happily, sometimes unhappily: she always leaves some kind of mark, wherefore listen cautiously to the admirer, yet more cautiously to the tattler. It requires the whole attention at such times, to discover the intent of the newsbearer, in order to know beforehand which foot he is going to put forward. With reflection examine into what may be feigned, and what may be false.

ৡ **8 1** ৡ

KNOW HOW TO renew your glitter. It is the birthright of the Phoenix: even the best goes stale, and so its fame, for familiarity kills admiration, wherefore something fresh even though mediocre comes to outshine the greater virtue, grown old. Bring about, therefore, your rebirth, in courage, in spirit, in fortune, in everything. Clothe yourself anew in shining armor, and rise again like the sun: change the theatre for your appearance, in order that your absence from the one may evoke desire, and your novelty in the other, applause.

ৡ **8 2** ৡ

DRINK NOTHING TO the dregs, either of the bad, or of the good, for to moderation in everything has one sage reduced all wisdom. Too great justice becomes injustice, and the orange, squeezed too hard, turns bitter: even in enjoyment, do not go too far. The spirit itself grows weary if worked too long, and he draws blood instead of milk, who milks too hard.

ᏁᏳ **8 3** ᏜᎳ

ALLOW YOURSELF SOME pardonable defect;
for a certain weakness at times may be the greatest
evidence of strength. Envy carries its ostracisms, just as
civil, as they are criminal: it accuses the most holy of
sin, because without sin; and because totally perfect,
condemns totally. Envy makes of itself an Argus to discover the flaws of the flawless, for its own comfort.
Detraction like lightning, only strikes the greatest
heights. At such times, therefore, let Homer sleep, and
let him affect some lack of spirit, or of virtue; but not
of prudence, in order to appease envy, that it burst not
of its own poison: wave a cloak before the bull of jealousy, to rescue immortality.

ᏁᏳ **8 4** ᏜᎳ

KNOW HOW TO profit through your enemies.
Learn how to grasp a thing, not by its blade
which cuts, but by its hilt, which protects: especially in
the battle of life. To a wise man, his enemies avail him
more, than to a fool, his friends. Evil intent often levels
a mountain of difficulty, which the best intent in the
world could not hope to climb over. Many have been
made through the greatness of their enemies. Far more
to be feared is flattery, than hate, since this exposes the
flaws, which flattery would conceal. The man who

knows makes a mirror of spite, more faithful than the mirror of affection, and envisages his shortcomings, to correct them, for prudence grows apace, when it must live against rivalry, or malevolence.

࿔ **8 5** ࿔

D O NOT BE the ace; the fault of all that is best, that its overuse comes to be its misuse: the cry of all for it, comes to be the cry of all against it: a great misfortune, to be good for nothing, but not a lesser to be good for everything: such men end losers in spite of all they win, and live to be as despised, as once they were desired. The aces of every kind become dog-eared through overplay, and having fallen from the high estimation in which once they were held, they are consigned to the class of the common. The one protection against either extreme, is to hold to a middle place in the limelight, letting the superb in you reside in your qualifications, and not in your show of them; the brighter the torch, the quicker its burning, and the sooner its end; the fewer the performances, the higher the price paid for admission.

᳟ 8 6 ᳟

FORESTALL EVIL GOSSIP. The mob has many heads, and therefore many eyes for malice, and many tongues for slander. Let it start to gossip, and the greatest reputation is sullied; let it develop a catchword, and an honored name is blotted out; the thing commonly starts from some visible defect, in some ridiculous weakness, that lends itself easily to a tale. And sometimes it is the prying malice of a rival, that feeds the mob; for there are hissers of malevolence, and they demolish a reputation most quickly with a jeer and a gibe. It is easy to give a man an evil name, because evil is gladly believed, but it takes much to blot it out. Wherefore the man of intelligence guards himself against such accident, by pitting his caution against the popular insolence, for it is easier to keep out, than to get out of trouble.

᳟ 8 7 ᳟

CULTURE, AND POLISH. Man is born the barbarian, and only culture redeems him from the bestial. Culture makes the man, and in its proportion. In this faith, could Greece call the rest of the world barbarous. Ignorance is rough: and nothing refines more than learning. But even this learning remains a crude affair, if sloven. Not only does our understanding require polish, but our desires as well, and especially our conduct. Some men are naturally polished, of courtly mien within and without, in thought and speech, and in bodily dress, which may be compared to the bark of a tree, as their gifts of the spirit may be likened to its fruit. Others are as naturally unpolished, so that all they have, even to their good points, seems eternally soiled by something unbearable.

ᔆ 8 8 ᔆ

GENEROUS IN ACTION, to attain nobility. The great man may not be small in his actions. He must not draw too fine distinctions, least of all in matters trivial: for even though it is well to take in everything, it is not so well to seem to peer into everything. Go at the day's work in that large spirit, which is the mark of gallantry. The great law in government is tolerance; most things should be allowed to pass unnoticed between intimates, between friends, and particularly between enemies. All stickling is a vexation of the spirit, and a burden to the soul. To return, time after time, to the same annoyance, is a sort of insanity, and so the way in which a man deports himself, is very likely to be the measure of his heart, and his mind.

ॐ 8 9 ॐ

A JUST ESTIMATE of yourself. Of your spirit, of your mind, of your judgment, of your passion. No man can be master of himself, who does not first understand himself. There are mirrors for the countenance, but none for the soul: wherefore make one out of the careful consideration of yourself, and while it may be well to forget the outer image, remember the inner, in order to fill out its defects, to make it better. Poll the powers of your mind, and of your will, in order to achieve something: take stock of what temper you have for the business of the day: sound your depths, and measure your capacity for everything.

ॐ 9 0 ॐ

THE ART OF living well. Of living abundantly! Two are done quickly with life, the fool, and the dissolute. The one because he does not know how to preserve it, and the other because he does not know its value. As virtue is its own reward; so is vice its own punishment: for he who lives too fast is quickly through, and in a double sense: while he who rests in virtue, never dies. For the life of the spirit becomes the life of the body, and the life lived well gathers unto itself not only fullness of days, but even length.

❦ 9 1 ❦

PROCEED ONLY WHEN without misgivings. The mere fear of failure in the executioner, is already its certainty in the observer, especially if he be a rival. If judgment had its doubts even in the heat of passion, it will later, when freed from such passion, condemn utterly and declare stupid the whole enterprise. Every undertaking of which you question the prudence, is dangerous, and safety lies in leaving it alone. Wisdom does not debate possibilities: it walks only in the noonday light of the intelligence. How can any venture come off well, which even in its conception was questioned by reason? and if plans unanimously passed upon by our very souls have a way of ending unhappily, what may be expected of those conceived of a hesitant mind, and divined to be bad by the judgment?

❦ 9 2 ❦

OF BETTER SENSE, I say, in everything. It is the first, and the greatest rule in work, and in speech; particularly for those who occupy the greatest, and the highest offices: of larger weight, one grain of common sense, than a bushel of cunning. It is the highroad to peace, though not so filled with cheers; even if the reputation of being wise is the triumph of fame, let it suffice you to have satisfied those who have understanding, for their judgment is the touchstone of what is well done.

༄ **9 3** ༅

A N ALL-ROUND MAN. To be a man of many sides, is to count as many men. He makes life richer, by bestowing his wealth upon his neighborhood. Variety in what is best, is the joy of life. A great art, that of knowing how to garner all that is good: and since nature has made in man an epitome of herself, by giving him highest standing, let art make him into a little universe through the exercise, and the development of his taste and of his mind.

༄ **9 4** ༅

O F UNMEASURED CAPACITY. A watchful man will decline to be plumbed to the depths, be it of his knowledge, or of his powers, if he would remain esteemed: let him allow himself to be known, but not to the point of being comprehended. Permit no one to discover the limits of your capacities, because of the obvious danger of disillusionment. Never suffer another to see through you completely: for surmise and supposition regarding the talents of any man win greater respect, than definite knowledge thereof, no matter how great they be.

৯ **9 5** ৯

KNOW HOW TO keep anticipation alive: always striving to feed it, by letting the much promise more, and the one achievement be the announcement only of a greater. Put not all your reserves into the first throw; the great trick is to dole out strength, and to dole out mind, in such fashion as to bring forward increasingly the fulfillment of what was expected of you.

৯ **9 6** ৯

HAVE SOUL, FOR it is the shrine of reason, the foundation of prudence, and its faith makes easy the attainment of every goal. It is a gift from heaven, and the most to be desired, because heaven's first, and its greatest. It is the very breastplate of armor, and so much so, that nothing else a man may lack will allow him to be called not a man, but only a richer or poorer one. All the activities of life depend upon its influence; and all beg its good opinion, for everything must pass in judgment before it. It consists of an inborn love for all that conforms most to reason, marrying always with that which is most true.

৯ **9 7** ৯

A TTAIN, AND MAINTAIN a reputation, for it is the usufruct of fame. A stiff climb, for it is the issue of excellence, as rare as mediocrity is common. But once attained, it is easily maintained. It asks for much, but it yields more. When it rises to the height of veneration, it becomes a kind of majesty; either because of the holiness of its cause, or of its influence; but only the reputation well founded endures forever.

৯ **9 8** ৯

H IDE YOUR PURPOSE. The passions are the windows of the soul. And practical wisdom calls for acting. He hazards defeat who plays with cards exposed. Pit the defence of caution, against the offence of the adversary; against the eye of the lynx, the ink of the cuttlefish. Even our wishes must not be voiced, so that they may not be met, by the one to deny them, or by another to satisfy them.

৯ **9 9** ৯

T HE REAL, AND the apparent. Things do not count for what they are, but for what they seem; they are few who look into the depths, and they are many who are satisfied to pay at face. It is not sufficient even to be right if it carry the face of being wrong.

ᎤᎦ **1 0 0** ᎤᎦ

A MAN WITHOUT bias, a thinking Christian. A world philosopher, who does not merely appear such, much less affect to be such. Philosophy stands discredited today, even though once the major pursuit of the sages. The science of the thinker lives degraded. Seneca introduced it into Rome; it found favor for a time in the courts, but today it is reckoned nonsense. And yet the detection of error was ever the food of the thinking spirit, and the joy of the righteous.

ᎤᎦ **1 0 1** ᎤᎦ

H ALF THE WORLD laughs at the other half, even though the lot are fools. Either everything is good, or everything is bad, depending on the vote; what one sues, another pursues. An insufferable fool, he who wishes the universe regulated according to his plans. Bliss does not derive from the pleasure of any one man: for there are as many minds, as there are heads, and as different; there is no weakness without its admirer, so be not discomfited because your ways displease some, for they will not fail to be pleasing to others: nor let their approval of them make you vain, for still others will condemn them. Proper satisfaction may be taken only in the approval of men of authority, and by those who have standing in their fields. Do not live by the sanction of any one voice, or of any one custom, or of any single period.

ஜ *1 0 2* ஜ

A MAW FOR large slices of fortune. In the great body of wisdom, an organ of no minor importance is a great craw, for every great corpus must needs be composed of great parts. He will not be gorged by good fortune, who is worthy of more, for what is indigestion to one, is only appetite to another. There are many, who turn sick whenever the food is rich, because they are naturally weak, being neither accustomed to, nor born to high living; the business sours on them, and from the fumes arising out of their unearned distinction, they go dizzy in the head; they run great danger in their high places, unable to maintain themselves in them, because unaccustomed. Wherefore, let the really big man evidence that he has the capacity for even larger enterprise, and avoid with special care all show of anything that indicates faint heart.

❧ 1 0 3 ❧

EACH, IN HIS way, majestic. Every man's actions, even if not those of a king, should be worthy of such, and according to his station, his ways regal within the limits of his gifts. Greatness in action, loftiness of mind, in everything he does, mark the king by merit, if not by birth, for true sovereignty lies in perfection of conduct; no need for a king to begrudge another a grandeur of which he is the prototype, especially in those deputed to the throne, for something of this truly sovereign quality should stick to them, only let them, not merely assume the attributes of majesty, in vain ceremony, and grow pompous, but let them realize these within themselves.

❧ 1 0 4 ❧

KNOW WHAT THE offices hold. There is variety to them, and it takes a magistrate's mind to know their values, yet nothing calls for greater care in choice; some demand courage, and others shrewdness. It is most easy to manage in those which call merely for honesty, and most difficult in those which call for skill. With decent endowment nothing else is necessary for the former: but for the latter, all ardor may not suffice, and sleeplessness. A wearying business to govern man, and these mostly cracked, or fools: for double brains are needed with those who have none. Most intolerable are those posts which require the whole of a man, for set hours, and at set tasks; better are those freer from weariness, wherein the serious is joined to variety: because change refreshes the spirit. The most to be desired are such which carry a measure of independence; and those are the worst, which sweat a man to death in his human frame, and yet more in his divine.

༃ 1 0 5 ༂

NOT A BORE. The man of one business, or of one speech gets heavy. Brevity charms, and better accomplishes the daily course; it makes up in manner, what it lacks in measure. The good, if short, is doubly good; and even the bad, if brief, is not so bad. The essence is always stronger than the lees: and it is common knowledge, that the man longwinded is rarely wise, either in what he has at disposal, or in the form of the disposal. There are men who serve more to encumber, than to adorn this world, mere tinsel that everybody pushes aside. A man of discernment will avoid making himself a nuisance, especially to the great, for they are much occupied, and it is worse to annoy any one of them, than the rest of the world put together. What is well said is said quickly.

❧ 1 0 6 ❧

D O NOT MAKE a show of what you have. More offensive to boast your social position than your qualifications; to make yourself the central figure is to make yourself envied, and one should have enough of hate. Deference is the less likely to be gained, the harder it is pursued, for respect depends upon others; and so one cannot snatch but only merit it, and wait: large offices demand distinction in their exercise, without which they are not worthily administered, wherefore maintain in them the dignity necessary to the proper discharge of their obligations: not insisting upon respect, but yourself compelling it, for all who trade upon their offices, show that they do not merit them, and that they are not big enough for the honor; if you would be important, let it be through the excellence of your talents, rather than through your position; for even a king should be worshipped, more because of his qualifications, than because of the accident of his birth.

❧ 1 0 7 ❧

D ISPLAY NO SELF-SATISFACTION. Live, not unsatisfied with yourself, for that is cowardice, nor yet self-satisfied, for that is stupidity. Self-complacency starts for the most part in witlessness, and ends in a blissful ignorance which even though soothing to the soul, does not maintain a name. Because unable to equal the great qualifications of another, you are content with some vulgar mediocrity within yourself. Always more useful and more intelligent to have misgivings about yourself, either for your better assurance that things will come off well, or for your better comfort if they come off badly; for he cannot be surprised by a turn of luck, who has already feared it. Homer himself must sleep at times, and Alexander come down from his pedestal and out of his delusion. Things depend upon many circumstances, and what was a triumph in one place, and upon that occasion, in another becomes a disgrace, but what is most unruly about this form of stupidity is that complacency flowers, and then buds forth all about through its seeds.

ঽৌ *1 O 8* ৰ্জ

THE SHORTEST ROAD to being somebody is to know whom to follow. Contact is the most effective way in which to learn manner, and taste: one thus takes on the thought, and even the spirit of others without being aware of it. Wherefore, let the intemperate join up with those more temperate; and so with the rest of the mental attributes, that the man of moderation may be brought forth without violence: a great trick to know how to adapt yourself. The play of contrasts makes beautiful this universe, and sustains her, and if it will bring about such harmony in the physical world, it will accomplish an even greater in the moral. Avail yourself of this courteous admonition in the choice of your friends, and your fellows, so that through the meetings of the extremes, there may arise a most sensible mean.

ঀ *1 0 9* ঀ

NOT THE VILLAGE constable. There are men of evil mind, who would make of everything a crime, and not because of passion, but just naturally. They condemn everybody, some for what they have done, and others for what they may do. It is the sign of a narrow mind, as cruel as it is vile, for they charge so immoderately, that of motes they fashion beams with which to put out the eyes. Slave drivers in every position, they would make a galley of what was an elysium; for in the midst of excitement, they push everything to extremes. The large soul, on the other hand, finds an excuse for everything, if not in intention, then in inattention.

ঀ *1 1 0* ঀ

DO NOT WAIT to be the sun, in her setting. A maxim of the wise, to leave before being left. Know how to make a triumph even of your exit; for at times the sun herself when most bright, will retire behind a cloud, that she may not be seen to sink, thus to leave us in doubt as to whether she has set, or has not set. Escape such accident, in order not to suffer slight; do not wait until men turn their backs upon you, that they bury you, still alive in your feelings, but dead in their estimation: the man of foresight puts his horse in the stable betimes, and does not wait to see it create laughter by falling in the middle of the race: the beauty wisely cracks her mirror when it is yet early, not to do it with impatience later when it has disillusioned her.

?§ *111* ?§

HAVE FRIENDS. It is a second life. Every friend is something good, and something wise to his friend: and between them everything comes off well; a man is only worth, what the others will him; and that they may will him much, the way must be found to their hearts: there is no magic like that of friendly service; and the best way to have friends, is to make them: the most, and the best of what is ours, depends upon others: we have to live, either with friends, or with enemies, wherefore try daily to make a friend, and even if not as an intimate, at least as one well disposed, that some may remain afterwards as confidants having passed the ordeal of selection.

⚘ *1 1 2* ⚘

GAIN GOOD WILL; for God himself allows it to enter into His greatest designs, and gives it place. Through it is won a favorable disposition: and some have such faith in its virtue, that they hold diligence cheap, because the man alert knows well that the path of mere merit is a stony one, if he is not helped along by good will: for it eases and aids everything, not always supposing the existence of great virtues, but imposing them, like courage, honesty, learning and even conscience: and failing to see all shortcomings, because it does not wish to see them: ordinarily it springs from mere alikeness in material interests, as those of the body, the nation, the family, the country or the profession: but in its deeper form it is more noble: having to do then with the talents, character, fame, merit; all the difficulty lies in arousing good will, for its maintenance is easy, but good will can be won, and its power should be known.

⚘ *1 1 3* ⚘

PREPARE YOURSELF IN good fortune, for the bad. Expedient in the summer to make provision for the winter, and much more convenient; at that time good will comes cheap, and friends are plentiful; well then to garner the two against bad times, when adversity shows her face, and all things fail. Gather up your friends, and the men beholden to you, for someday you may have appreciation for what today you have no place. The base have no friends in their prosperity because they do not know them; and not in their adversity because they are disavowed by them.

ༀ 114 ༀ

NEVER THE CHEAP rival. Every effort to outshine an opponent lowers the standing, for competition resorts at once to mudslinging, in order to besmirch. They are few who carry on war in fair fashion, for rivalry lays bare the flaws which courtesy has covered over: many lived in honor, as long as they had no emulators. The heat of combat calls up, and brings to life infamies long dead, and digs up stenches forgotten: competition starts with a manifesto of slander, and calls to its aid whatever it can, and not what it should; and when at times, nay mostly, insults prove not the arms of victory, these men find a vile satisfaction in their spite, and bandy it about with so much air, that the dust of forgetfulness is shaken from old scandals. Men of good will were ever men of peace, and men of honor, men of good will.

❧ 1 1 5 ❧

ACCUSTOM YOURSELF TO the defects of those about you, as you would accustom yourself to those of ugly face, it being the best way out when you are a subordinate, for there are beasts, with whom no one can live, nor yet without. It is, therefore, the part of wisdom to get used to them as to ugliness itself, in order that on some terrible occasion you may not forget yourself. When first seen they terrify, but little by little this fear grows less, and reflection hardens against the unpleasant, or learns how to bear it.

❧ 1 1 6 ❧

DEAL SOLELY WITH men of honor: with such only may you be involved, and such only may you involve. What they have done is best pledge of what they will do, even in the business of shuffling the cards, for they deal above board, and so it avails more to lose with men of honor, than to win with men of dishonor, for there is no profit in crookedness, because it is unbeholden to honesty; on this account there is no true friendship among thieves; nor are their protestations of friendship true, even when they seem it, for they are not made in good faith; and those without such should ever be abnominated of men, for they who do not cherish honor, do not cherish virtue, and honor is the throne of virtue.

৯৯ *117* ৯৯

NEVER TALK ABOUT yourself. For you either praise, which is vanity, or you repproach, which is poor spirit, in both instances evincing a guilty heart in the speaker, which gives pain to the listener: if it is to be avoided in private life, it is to be shunned even more in public office, where you speak to the crowd, and where you at once pass as a fool if you but give the semblance of it. A similar weakness of mind lies in speech about those present, because of the danger of foundering on either of two rocks, that of overappreciation, or that of depreciation.

৯৯ *118* ৯৯

GAIN THE NAME of being a gentleman, for it is enough to make you loved. Courtesy is the stem of culture, a species of sorcery, and so gains the affection of everybody, just as discourtesy wins scorn, and universal hatred; when discourtesy is born of arrogance, it is abominable; when of coarseness, detestable. Let courtesy always be too much, rather than too little, but let it not be equal, lest it degenerate into unfairness: hold to it as a matter of duty between enemies, for it exhibits your courage, costing little, and being worth much, for to show honor is to be honored. Gallantry, and honor have this advantage, they are saved through being spent, the first if practiced, the second if worn.

๕ **119** ๖

DO NOT MAKE yourself something hated. Do not provoke hatred, for even without invitation, it will come quickly enough. There are many who hate gratis, without knowing why, or wherefore; ill will has a way of outdistancting good will: for the urge in us to injure another is more potent, and swifter than the desire to advantage ourselves. Some are happy only when at outs with everybody, either because vexed, or to vex; and when hate has once taken hold of a man, it is as hard to get rid of, as a bad reputation. Men of clear judgment are feared, the evil-tongued are abhorred; the presumptuous make sick, the buffoons are detested, and the singular are left to themselves. Try, therefore, to show appreciation in order to be appreciated; and let him who desires affection, show affection.

๕ **120** ๖

LIVE ACCORDING TO the custom. Even wisdom must be in style, and where it is not, it is well to know how to feign ignorance, for thought and taste change with the times: do not be old-fashioned in thought, and modern in taste. The choice of the many carries the vote in every field. For the time being, therefore, it must be bowed to, in order to bring it to higher level: the man of wisdom accommodates himself to the present, even though the past seems better, alike in the dress of his spirit, as in the dress of his body. Only in the matter of being decent does this rule of life not apply, for virtue should be practiced eternally: yet today it is unknown, and to speak the truth and to keep one's word, seem the marks of another age: and good men appear the creations of a good time that is past; but they are forever loved: if by chance, some be still left, they are no longer in style, and no longer imitated. Oh, the misery of this our age, which holds virtue alien, and evil the order of the day! Let the man of conscience live as he can, not as he might wish. Let him hold as better what fortune has conceded him than what she has denied him.

⇜ 1 2 1 ⇝

DO NOT MAKE a business of the trivial. Just as some can make a tale out of anything, so others can make a business of everything: they always speak importantly, they take all things seriously, making of everything either a case, or a mystery. To convert petty annoyances into matters of importance, is to become seriously involved in nothing. It is to miss the point, to carry on the chest what has been cast from the shoulders. Many things which were something, by being left alone became nothing; and others which were nothing, became much because messed into: in its beginnings it is easy to make an end of anything, but not so, later; for many a time the remedy itself brings out the disease: by no means the worst rule of life, to let things rest.

༃ 1 2 2 ༃

DISTINCTION, IN SPEECH and in action. It makes a large place for itself everywhere, and compels respect in advance; showing itself in everything, in bearing, in talk, at times in the walk, or even in the look, and in the desire. A great triumph, thus to win all hearts, for it is not the fruit of a silly frowardness, or of a stupid superciliousness, but of a becoming authority, born of a superior mind, and helped along by merit.

༃ 1 2 3 ༃

A MAN WITHOUT AFFECTATION. The greater your qualifications, the less the need to affect any of them, for this vulgarly insults all the rest. Affectation is as distasteful to everybody else, as it is painful to him who practices it, for he lives a martyr to apprehension, and is tormented by punctiliousness; the greatest virtues lose their merit when believed the children of violence, rather than those of innocence, since all that is natural is always more pleasing, than the artificial. The affected will always be held foreign to him who feigns it; the better a thing is done, the less must it betray effort, because the perfect must appear as fallen ready-made from heaven; nor, in order to escape affectation, become affected in trying not to be: the man of discrimination never exhibits his virtues, for it is through their very concealment that they awaken the interest of others. Twice great is he who carries all his perfections within himself, and none in his own conceit, and via by-path thus reaches the goal of approbation.

༔ 1 2 4 ༔

S TRIVE TO BE in demand. Few attain to such grace in the eyes of men, and if these be men of understanding, joy, indeed; for coldness is the rule toward those who have done; but there are ways of gaining this prize of adoration; excellence in a post, and excellence of the talents assure it, and charm of manner is efficacious, for eminence is built upon such properties, because of which it is soon discovered that the man needed the office less than the office needed the man; the posts bring honor to some men, and other men bring honor to their posts: but there is no glory in being held good, because he who succeeded you is bad, for this does not prove that you are wanted back, but only that the other is wanted out.

❧ 1 2 5 ❧

NOT THE POLICE-COURT blotter. The sign of blemish in yourself, to point to the shame of another: some seek with the spots of others to cover their own, either to white-wash them, or thus to console themselves, which is the solace of fools: the breath smells badly from those who are the sewers of a city's filth, in which stuff he who digs deepest, soils himself most: few are free from some original sin, be it of commission, or omission, only, the sins of little known people are little known; let the man alert guard against being a recorder of evil, for it is to be a man despised, and one who even though human, is inhuman.

❧ 1 2 6 ❧

HE IS NOT a fool who commits foolishness, but he who having done so does not know how to conceal it. If your merits should be kept under seal, how much more your demerits. All man go wrong; but with this difference, the intelligent cover up what they have committed, and the fools expose even what they may commit. A good name rests more upon what is concealed, than upon what is revealed, for he who cannot be good, must be cautious: the sins of great men should be regarded as mere eclipses of the heavenly bodies. Let it be a mistake to confide your errors even to a friend, for were it possible, you should not disclose them to yourself; but since this is impossible, make use here of that other principle of life, which is: learn how to forget.

৯৫ **1 2 7** ৯৫

A CHARM IN EVERYTHING. It is the life of the talents, the flower of speech, the soul of action, the halo of splendor itself: every other grace is the apparel merely of nature, but charm is the ornament of grace itself, showing even in the daily round; for the most part it is a bequest of fortune, owing little to schooling, to which it is superior; being more than ease, and approaching daring, it takes unembarrassment for granted, and adds perfection to performance; without it all beauty is dead, and all grace, graceless, for it transcends courage, wisdom, prudence, majesty itself. It is the courteous way about in every business, and the polite way out of every embarrassment.

৯৫ **1 2 8** ৯৫

OF LOFTY AMBITION. The first requisite to make the hero, because it spurs him to every species of greater attainment, improving his taste, quickening his heart, stimulating his mind, ennobling his spirit, and dignifying his majesty: whatever it settles upon it glorifies, and even when at times the bitterness of fate brings defeat, it returns anew to the conflict, strengthened in will, even as it was frustrated in accomplishment: magnanimity, generosity, and every heroic virtue recognize in it their source.

৯৯ *1 2 9* ৯৯

NEVER CRY ABOUT your woes. To make lamentation only discredits you; to better purpose, to be an example of boldness against passion, than one of timidity under compassion; to lament is to open the way to the listener, to the very thing of which you complain, and by giving notice of a first insult, making excuse for a second; many a man with his complaint of injustices past, has invited more, and by crying for help, or for pity, has merely gained sufferance; or even contempt: better politics, to laud the generosity of one, thus to lay obligations upon another; for to recite the favors done by those absent, is to compel them from those present, for this is to sell the esteem in which you are held by the one, to the other; and so a man of sense will never publish abroad, either the slights, or the wrongs he may have suffered, but only the honor in which he is held, for it will serve better to constrain his friends, and to restrain his enemies.

❧ 1 3 0 ❧

D O, AND EXHIBIT your doing. Things do not pass for what they are, but for what they seem: to have worth, and to know how to show it, is to be worth double; that which is not made apparent is as though it were not, for even justice is not venerated, unless it carry the face of justice; those who are fooled, outnumber those who are not: for it is sham that rules, and things are judged by what they look, even though most things are far different from what they appear; a good exterior is the best recommendation of the excellence of the interior.

❧ 1 3 1 ❧

G REATNESS OF FEELING. The soul has its courage, a gallantry of the spirit, which lifts up the heart, not found in all men, because it calls for magnanimity: its first affair is to speak well of an enemy, and to deal with him even better: it shines most brightly in moments most opportune for revenge, when, instead of ignoring them, it brings them into higher relief, by converting victory into an unexpected generosity. Even so it remains politic, yea, the flower of diplomacy, never displaying triumph, because it displays nothing, and although merit attained it, modestly concealing the fact.

ఇ§ 1 3 2 ఆ§

K NOW THE VALUE of reconsideration. To appeal for review, makes for safety, and especially where disatisfaction is evident, to gain time, either to soften judgment, or to strengthen it. New reasons appear to support and to confirm the decision; if something is to be granted, then the gift well considered is cherished more than that bestowed in the rush of the moment; for what has been longed for, is always prized more highly, and if something must be refused, time gives opportunity for discovering how best, and most softly, to say No; that it be better flavored, and usually when the first heat of desire has passed off, the disappointment of refusal appears less cold-blooded; to him who pleads too urgently, concession should always be made tardily, for that trick discovers the blow-holes.

ఇ§ 1 3 3 ఆ§

B ETTER A FOOL with the crowd, than a sage by yourself; the politicians say, that if all men are fools, no one of them can be counted such; wherefore the wise man who stands apart, must be a fool: it is important therefore to go with the current: the greatest knowledge at times, to know nothing, or to affect to know nothing; we have to live with others, and the stupid make up the majority; to live alone one must have within himself, either much of God, or much of the beast: I am strongly urged to turn this aphorism about, and say: better wise with the rest of the wise, than a fool by yourself: still some find distinction in making fools of themselves.

ৰ্জ 1 3 4 ৰু

POSSESS YOURSELF OF the necessities of life twice over. It is to insure doubly your existence, for you may not depend solely upon, or be limited to, any one thing, however extraordinary it may be; everything should be had twice over, and especially the means of life, good will, and satisfaction. The face of the moon changes constantly even though it rests upon the permanent; how much more do the things of this life, which depend upon a human charity, that is most fragile. Lay up against this brittleness a reserve, and let it be the policy of your life, to have in double store the means for living well, and comfortably; just as nature has given us doubly of those members which are most important, and most exposed, so let art assure us doubly of those things upon which life itself depends.

ৰ্জ 1 3 5 ৰু

DO NOT CARRY a spirit of contradiction, for it is to be freighted with stupidity, and with peevishness, and your intelligence should plot against it; though it may well be the mark of mental genius to see objection, a wrangler about everything cannot escape being marked the fool, for he makes guerrilla warfare of quiet conversation, and so becomes more of an enemy to his intimates, than to those with whom he will have nothing to do; it is in the most savoury morsel that the spine which gets caught hurts most, and so it is with contradiction in moments of happy converse; such a man is a fool, offensive, who adds to the untamed within himself, the beastly.

ॐ *1 3 6* ॐ

PUT YOURSELF IN the middle of things, to get at once at the heart of the business; most roam around, in useless millings either about the edge, or in the scrub of a tiresome verbosity, without striking upon the substance of the matter; they make a hundred turns about a point, wearying themselves, and wearying others, yet never arriving at the centre of what is important; it is the product of a scattered brain that does not know how to get itself together; they spend time, and exhaust patience, over that which they should leave alone, and afterwards are short of both for what they did leave alone.

ॐ 1 3 7 ॐ

L ET THE WISE man be sufficient unto himself. He who was all in all to himself, when carrying himself hence, carried everything with him. If one learned friend can rebuild for you Rome, and all the rest of the world: be such a friend to yourself, and you will be able to live alone: for to whom might you be beholden, when there exists no better mind, and no better judgment than your own? Learn to rely upon yourself, because it makes for that happy supremacy which is like the supremacy of the Highest. He who is thus able to live within himself, is like the brute in nothing, like the sage in much, and like God in everything.

ॐ 1 3 8 ॐ

T HE SENSE TO let things settle. Especially when the public, or the private, sea is most turbulent. There come whirlwinds into human traffic, storms of passion, when it is wise to seek a safe harbor with smoother waters: many times is an evil made worse by the remedies used; here leave things to nature, or there to God: the learned physician needs just as much wisdom in order not to prescribe, as to prescribe, and often the greater art lies in doing nothing; the way to quiet the turbulence of a mob is to withdraw your hand, and let it quiet itself, to concede today, may be the best way to succeed tomorrow; it takes little to muddy a spring, nor does it clear by being stirred, but by being left alone: there is no better remedy for turmoil, than to let it take its course, for so it comes to rest of itself.

ൠ *1 3 9* ൠ

K NOW YOUR UNLUCKY days: for such there are, when nothing goes right, and even though the game change, the bad luck does not: you know them after two throws of the dice, and you retire, or play on, depending upon whether this is such a day, or not. Even the mind has its periods, for no man is wise at all hours, since it takes luck to think straight, just as it takes luck to write a good letter, for all good things have their season, beauty not always being in style, judgment itself turning traitor, now making us too soft, now too harsh: thus anything to come off well, must be of its day. Just so does everything go wrong with some, and everything go right with others, and with less effort. All they touch stands ready, the spirit is well-disposed, the mind is alert, and their star is in the ascendant. Then is the hour to strike, and not to squander the least advantage. But the man of judgment will not let just one throw augur the day unlucky, or lucky, for the former may have been only mischance, and the latter only happy accident.

﷽ 140 ﷽

HIT AT ONCE upon the good in everything. It is the reward of good taste: the bee goes directly to the sweet for its comb, and the adder to the bitter for its venom. And so with the tastes of men, some to the good, some to the bad: there is nothing that does not hold some good, especially if it be a book, because of the thought it may contain: but the minds of some men are of such unhappy frame, that out of a thousand good points they strike upon the lone bad, and this they trot out and carp upon, mere scavengers of the soil of other men's purposes, and minds, and mere compilers of the sins of others; better punishment for their bad choice, than occupation for their cleverness; they lead a sad life, for they batten forever on the bitter, and make bread of refuse; happier the taste of those, who among a thousand evils strike at once upon the single good, even though present only by chance.

﷽ 141 ﷽

NOT INFATUATED WITH your own voice. Small comfort to be satisfied with yourself, if you do not satisfy others, and general disdain usually punishes such conceit; he owes everybody who would pay by personal note, for to wish to be the speaker, and the auditor too, does not go well; if to talk to yourself is nonsense, to wish to listen to yourself and this before others, is nonsense twice over. It is the habit of these gentlemen to speak to some such refrain as, I am about to say, or, Ahem, all torture to those who must listen; every moment they strain the ear for approbation, or flattery, to drive men crazy. The inflated always mouth other men's words, and as their talk parades in the buskins of arrogance, their every word calls forth the stupid approval of some fool: Well said!

ॐ *1* 4 *2* ॐ

NEVER OUT OF stubbornness hold to the wrong side, just because your adversary anticipated you, and chose the right, for then you are beaten from the start and will have to retire in disgrace; the right is never saved through the wrong; the opponent was clever to preëmpt the better side and you stupid to oppose him by taking up the worse: stubbornness in action is more ensnarling than stubbornness in speech, for there is greater risk in doing than in talking: the vulgarity of these clowns, that they observe not the truth, because they lie; nor yet their own interest, because on the wrong side. A heedful man stands always on the side of reason, and never that of passion, either because he foresaw it from the first, or found it better afterwards; for if the adversary is a fool he may on his own account change face, adopt the opposite side and so weaken his position; but the only way to drive him from the better side, is to seize it yourself, for his stupidity will make him drop it, and his obstinacy free you from your own.

❧ 143 ❧

NOT A SMART-ALECK, in order to escape being commonplace. Either extreme discredits you. Every act, that deviates from the serious, borders upon the foolish. A paradox in essence is a species of pious fraud, which is admired because of its freshness, and its piquancy; but later when its trickiness is discovered fares so badly, that it is scorned. It is a kind of imposition, and in political matters, the ruin of the state. Those who cannot, or those who dare not, do something really great over the road of merit, repair to the paradoxical, to be admired of fools, and to become a red-light to the prudent: it is the mark of a disordered judgment, and on this account should be forsworn by the discerning; and though at times it may not be founded upon error, it is rarely founded upon truth, to the great hazard of all that is important.

❧ 144 ❧

ENTER INTO THE plans of another in order to come out with your own. It is the strategic means to an end; even in heavenly matters, Christian fathers inculcate this holy principle. It is a great trick because it baits useful enterprise, by gaining goodwill, for while it looks as though his ends were being served, the manoeuvre serves no less to open the way to your own; but the business may not be entered upon by the bungler, especially where the ground is dangerous; wherefore, with persons whose first response inclines to be No, it is well to cover the play, in order that the difficulty of concession may not be observed, especially if it look like a reversal in judgment: this bit of advice belongs to those rules that have to do with action through indirection, all of which are exquisitely subtle.

ఇఇ 1 4 5 ఇఇ

DO NOT EXHIBIT your sore finger; for all to strike upon, and do not complain of it, for malice always pounds where it hurts most. No use to get angry, for this will only add to the general amusement: evil intent goes sneaking around to uncover the infirmity, and prods about to discover where the suffering is greatest, in a thousand different ways, until it hits the spot. Never will the circumspect reveal his feelings, or disclose his disease, be it acquired, or inherited, for fate herself is pleased at times to scourge us, and just where it pains most. She always mortifies us in the flesh, on which account never disclose, either what worries, or what refreshes, the one that it may pass, the other that it may last.

❧ 1 4 6 ❧

LOOK BENEATH. For ordinarily things are far other than they seem; and the dullness which does not seek to pass beyond the rind, is due to be increasingly disillusioned if it gets deeper into the interior. The false is forever the lead in everything, continually dragging along the fools: the truth brings up the rear, is late, and limps along upon the arm of time, wherefore the man of insight will save for it at least the half of that faculty, which our great mother has wisely given us twice. Deceit is superficial, wherefore the superficial are taken in at once. The man of substance lives safely within himself, to be better treasured of his colleagues, and of those who know.

❧ 1 4 7 ❧

OPEN TO SUGGESTION. None is so perfect, that he may not at times need a monitor, for he is incurably the fool who will not listen: even the most high should lend ear to friendly advice, for sovereignty itself may not shut off gentlemanly counsel: there are men who cannot be saved because they cannot be reached, who hurl themselves to destruction because none dares to approach to restrain them: the most faultless should leave open one door to friendship, for it may prove a portal of succor; place should be made for one friend at least to advise without embarrassment, and even to find fault; but this privilege should rest upon his rightness, and upon our trust in him, and his understanding: but we need not bare our inner selves to just anybody, not even our reputation; keep within the closet of your soul the faithful mirror of a trusted friend to whom you may turn, and from whom you will take correction when in error.

ᘏᕐᕐ 1 4 8 ᕬᕣ

HAVE THE ART of conversation, for it is the hallmark of the man. No human enterprise demands greater heed, for so large a part of everyday life, whence its dangers, or its advantages; if care is necessary to write a letter, which is conversation studied, and committed to paper; how much more is necessary in everyday speech, when the intelligence must at every moment pass examination? Men skilled, take the pulse of the soul at the tongue, in which knowledge the Sage of sages said: Speak, if you would that I know you. Some hold that the art of conversation lies in its artlessness, that it should lack formality, like the clothing; this may hold between friends, but where it is to gain respect, it must have more form, to display better the substance of the man: to strike it right you must be able to adapt yourself to the mind, and to the spirit of your company; do not make yourself a carping critic of words, or you will be held the grammatical fool; nor yet the opponent of what is reasonable, or all men will flee you, and look doubtfully upon what you have to say. Discretion in what is said, is better far than eloquence.

ॐ **1 4 9** ॐ

KNOW HOW TO let the blame slip upon another: to carry a shield against malevolence, is the wise strategy of those who govern, a thing not born of weakness, as the envious think, but of greater strength, to have on hand someone to shoulder the blame for failure, or to take on the punishment of general abuse: not everything can come off well; nor everybody be satisfied, wherefore provide yourself with someone to atone for your errors, and be a well for tears; even though it cost you some of your pride.

ॐ **1 5 0** ॐ

KNOW HOW TO sell your wares. Their intrinsic worth is not enough, for all do not turn the goods nor look deep; most run where the crowd is, running because the others run. It is a great art to know how to sell, at times by praising the goods, because praise excites desire, at times by giving them a good name, which is a great way to exalt them, but always cloaking any show of affectation in the matter. To say that they are intended for the sophisticated only, is to whet the public appetite, for everybody thinks himself sophisticated, and if he is not, then his sense of lack will spur on his desire: never should your business be accounted easy, or ordinary, for to make a thing easy is to make it common; all have an itch for the unusual because more desired alike by the taste and by the intelligence.

ᏚᏚ **1 5 1** ᏚᏚ

THINK AHEAD: today for tomorrow, and for many days beyond; the wisest of precautions, to take time for this: for to the ready there are no accidents, and to the forewarned no dangers: do not wait to think until you are overcome, but be forehanded: anticipate with matured reflection the worst outrages of destiny. The pillow is a silent Sibyl, and to sleep upon an enterprise, avails more than to be sleepless under it: some act first and think afterwards, which means they must concern themselves more with the excuses for, than the consequences of their acts: others think neither before, nor after, when all life should be continuous thinking, in order to hit upon the right way: it is reflection, and foresight that assure freedom to life.

ᏚᏚ **1 5 2** ᏚᏚ

NEVER ACCOMPANY HIM who puts you in the shade, either because more virtuous or more vicious: he of the greater capacity, gains the greater recognition: wherefore he will always play the main rôle, and you the second: and if any glory devolves upon you, it will be through his merits. The moon shines only when alone among the stars; for as the sun rises, it either fades, or goes out; never approach him who eclipses you, but only him who increases your lustre. It was by such means that the wise Fabula could look beautiful at the feast of Mars, and shine against the homeliness, and the slovenliness of her maids; neither endanger yourself by taking on the wrong side, nor grant honor to another at the cost of your own reputation; for to be made, walk with your superiors, but if made, with the mediocre.

153

BEWARE OF ENTERING to fill a great gap, but if you do commit yourself, let it be in the knowledge that you overfill it. It will be necessary to be worth double merely to seem to equal your predecessor. Just as it is wise, to see to it that he who succeeds you is such that you are wished back; it is similarly wise, to observe that he who preceded you does not eclipse you. A hard task to fill a great hiatus, for what has gone before always appears the better, wherefore to balance it does not suffice, because it holds the prior claim. It is therefore necessary to have command of additional gifts in order to dispossess the other of the higher opinion in which he is held.

ৰ্ঞ **1 5 4** ঞ্চ

SLOW TO BELIEVE, and slow to cherish. Maturity is recognized in the deliberateness with which a man adopts his creed: the false is the ordinary of the day, wherefore let belief be the extraordinary. He who is too quickly convinced, must too slowly become unconvinced; but do not exhibit your doubt in the faith of another, for that passes as discourtesy, or even insult, since such action holds your witness a cheat, or one cheated; even this however is not the greatest trouble, but that the unbeliever is marked the liar, since lying is burdened of two evils, it neither believes, nor is it believed. Suspension of judgment is always the part of wisdom in a listener, and the remission of faith to authority the part of wisdom in a speaker. Too ready allegiance is a kind of imprudence, for men lie in word, as they lie in deed, and the latter is more deadly because more active.

ৰ্ঞ **1 5 5** ঞ্চ

ART, IN RISING TO anger. Whenever possible, let cold deliberation take the place of sudden outburst; which should not prove difficult for him who has prudence. The first step in rising to anger, is to note that you are angry, for that is to enter master of the situation, having determined the need of it, and its height, and going no further; with this considered judgment let your wrath wax, and wane. Know well how to stop, and when, for the most difficult feat in racing lies in stopping. Fine proof of judgment to keep your head when the fools have lost theirs: every flare of temper is a step downwards from the rational; but properly checked it will not go beyond reason, or trample upon conscience: to be master of an angry mood, it is necessary always to ride with the tight rein of attention, and thus will you be the first man wise ahorse, if, indeed, not the last.

༜ 1 5 6 ༜

FRIENDS BY ELECTION. For they can be such only after they have been examined with discernment, and tested by time: the elect, not only of desire, but of judgment; though this be the most important deed in life, least care is exercised in its prosecution; intrusion brings some, but chance the most even though one is known by the friends he keeps, since he who is wise never consorts with fools; to find pleasure in a man does not prove him a friend, for this may spring more from the high value set upon his company, than upon the confidence felt in his capacity; there are friendships which are legitimate and others which are adulterous; the latter for your delight, the former to fructify your accomplishments: few are the friends of your self, the most, the friends of your success. The understanding of one good friend avails you more, than the good wishes of many others, wherefore let him be the product of choice, and not of accident. One wise friend knows how to relieve you of your burdens which the fool knows only how to put upon you; but do not wish him too good fortune, if you would not lose him.

᎒ᔕ *1 5 7* ᔕ᎒

D O NOT BE deceived in men, for it is the worst, and the easiest of deceptions; far better to be cheated in the price, than in the goods; nothing is more important than to look within: only there is a difference between knowing merchandise and knowing men; a great science to understand the minds of men, and to discern their humors: just as important to have studied men, as to have studied books.

᎒ᔕ *1 5 8* ᔕ᎒

K NOW HOW TO call forth the best in your friends. There is about this its own kind of good sense; some are good at a distance, and some nearby; and he, never easy in conversation may be in correspondence; for distance dulls shortcomings, intolerable at hand; a friend should not only bring satisfaction, but stimulation, for his are the three qualities of the good, by others called those of God: brotherliness, charity, and truth; for a friend is all in all; but few make good friends, and he who does not know how to choose them, makes fewer: to know how to keep friends is more than knowing how to make them. Search out those, who promise to last, and though at first they appear young, be content that they will grow old. The best variety undoubtedly are the salted, even though their digestion costs you a measure of effort. None lives so alone as he who lives without friends; for friendship doubles the good, and divides the bad; it is the only defense against misfortune, and the very balm of the spirit.

ᨅᨊ **1 5 9** ᨅᨊ

K NOW HOW TO suffer fools. The wise are always grouchy, for he who grows in wisdom, grows in impatience; he who knows much is harder to satisfy. The first precept of life, according to Epictetus: to be able to suffer; and to this may be reduced the half of all wisdom; if every type of folly must be borne, much patience will be required; at times we suffer most from those upon whom we most depend, which item is important because a school for self-control; out of suffering comes holy peace, which is the joy of the world; let him who cannot gain this state of forbearance take refuge within himself, if it be that he can stand even himself.

ૐ 1 6 0 ૐ

MARK YOUR WORDS, as a matter of caution when with rivals, and as a matter of decency, when with the rest. There is always time to add a word, but none in which to take one back: speak, therefore, as in a testament, for the fewer the words, the less the litigation: make of that which is of no importance the training ground for that which is: reserve has an aspect of divinity about it: he too easy of speech, shortly falters and falls.

ૐ 1 6 1 ૐ

KNOW YOUR PET failings. Even the man most perfect does not escape having some, to which he is either married, or with which he lives in concubinage: they live in the spirit, wherefore the greater this, the greater they, or the more apparent, tolerated not because their owner is unaware of them, but because he loves them: two evils joined, a passion, and a passion for something poor: they obscure the perfect, as offensive to the beholder, as sweet to the owner. Here is opportunity for self-conquest to make your talents shine forth more brightly; all men strike at once upon your shortcomings, so when they arrive to praise the great good in you which they admire, they are affronted to the disparagement of all your other gifts.

༐ 1 6 2 ༐

K NOW HOW TO triumph over the envious, and the malevolent. Not enough just to ignore them, even though courtesy is a great virtue; better to meet them with brave face, for there is not enough praise for him who speaks well of him who speaks ill; no vengeance more noble, than that which through worth, and ability, becomes the tormentor and the executioner of the envious: every success tightens the rope about the neck of the malevolent, and the glory of the envied becomes the hell of the envious; this is the greatest of all punishments, to be made unhappy by another's happiness: the envious dies not once, but as often as the envied is reborn by applause, the enduring fame of the one vying with the enduring torture of the other; for the envied is as immortal in his glory, as the envious is in pain. The trumpet of fame, which sounds the one to life eternal, brings execution to the other, sentenced to be choked to death by the choke of his envy.

༐ 1 6 3 ༐

N EVER THROUGH SORROW for their unhappiness involve yourself in the lot of the unfortunate. What is the bad luck of the one, may well be the good luck of the other, for the one could never be lucky, if many others were not unlucky; the characteristic of the unfortunate to win the favor of those gentlemen, who wish forever to make recompense by senseless charity, for the blows of unhappy fate, and so one sees at times him who in his prosperity was hated by all, in his adversity pitied by all: the hatred for the man exalted changed to a sympathy for the man cast down. Let the observant take note of how the cards of fortune are shuffled. There are some, who never walk except with the unfortunate, who are cheek by jowl today with the man in his unhappiness, from whom they fled yesterday in his happiness, all of which evidences nobility of the soul, but not of the intelligence.

ക 1 6 4 ക

STICK YOUR FINGER in the air. In order to discover how a matter will be received, especially if you suspect its success, or its sanction, for thus do you gain assurance of its happy outcome, or opportunity, either to go forward, or to turn back; you test out the public temper by this trick, and if observant learn where you stand, a good thing to know in law, in love, and in government.

ക 1 6 5 ക

MAKE A CLEAN fight. The man of intelligence may be driven to fight, but not to fight foully; each must act for what he is, and not for what he is held: to remain the gentlemen in a contest is to deserve all praise; fight to win, not only through superior strength, but through superior manner. To win basely, is not glorious, but humiliating. Always be the better in generosity; the knight does not avail himself of forbidden arms, and such are those of a friendship ended, for an enmity started, since one may not so convert a confidence into vengeance; all that smells of treason, corrupts a good name. Men of honor are affronted by the least atom of baseness; for the noble must be kept far from the vile. Glory in the fact that if gallantry, generosity, and fidelity were to perish off this earth, they would still be discoverable in your breast.

ৰঙ 1 6 6 ঙৰ

DISTINGUISH THE MAN of words from the man of deeds. It calls for rare judgment, as does distinction between friends, between persons, or between titles; for the difference is great; to be without good words or evil deeds is little; but to be without bad words or good deeds is less: we cannot feed on words, for they are the wind, nor can we live on mere manner, for that is polite sham; to hunt birds with a light, is truly to blind them. Let the pompous inflate themselves on bombast, but words should be the pledge of deeds, for herein lies their value; the trees that bear no fruit, but only leaves, are apt to lack heart; well to know them, to use the one for its timber, the other for its shade.

⚡ 1 6 7 ⚡

KNOW HOW TO help yourself. There is no better companion in the great struggles of life, than a stout heart; and when it flags it must be supported by the organs that stand about. Anxieties grow less in him who knows how to defend himself. Never surrender to fate, for then she ends by making herself intolerable. Some help themselves little with their burdens, in fact they double them because they do not know how to carry them. He who really knows himself, brings thought to the support of his frailties, wherefore the man of intelligence comes out victorious from under everything, even the unlucky stars.

⚡ 1 6 8 ⚡

DO NOT FALL into the class of the colossal asses. Such are all the pompous, the presumptuous, the stubborn, the capricious, the too easily led, the freaks, the affected, the facetious, the faddists, the perverse, the sectarians of all kinds, and the whole generation of the intemperate; monsters, all of them, of impertinence. Every distortion of the spirit, is more deforming than one of the body, because it degrades a superior beauty. But who can bring order out of such general confusion? Where the captain of the soul is missing, no use to look for direction; and what was meant as the gentle hint of derision, is falsely imagined to be applause.

༖ **1 6 9** ༖

A MISS COUNTS more than a hundred strikes.
None looks upon the sun in his splendor, but all in
his eclipse; vulgar history takes no count of what went
right, only of what went wrong; better known is all evil
through gossip, than all good through acclaim, for
many were never noticed until they failed; neither do
all the accomplishments of a man taken together avail
to blot out a single, and small failure; let every man get
himself clear in this matter, that cognizance will be
taken of everything he did badly, but none of what he
did well, by the tongue of slander.

༖ **1 7 0** ༖

IN ALL MATTERS keep something in reserve. It is to
insure your position; not all your wit must be spent
nor all your energies sapped every time; even of what
you know keep a rear guard, for it is to double your
advantage, always to have in reserve something to call
upon when danger threatens bad issue; the support
may mean more than the attack, because it exhibits
faith and fortitude. An intelligent man always plays
safe, wherefore even here that sharp paradox holds:
more is the half, than the whole.

ৰ্ক 1 7 1 ক্ষ

DO NOT SQUANDER favor. Great friends are for great occasions; so do not waste a great generosity upon a matter trivial, for that is to squander good will; let the holy anchor always be kept against the worst storm. If the great is spent upon the small, what will be left for afterwards? There is nothing more protective than a protector, nor anything more precious today than good will, for it makes, or unmakes the world, even to giving it life, or killing it. Men of wisdom, even as they are favored by nature, and by fame, are despised by fortune; wherefore it marks their better judgment to have, and to hold friends, than chattels.

ৰ্ক 1 7 2 ক্ষ

DO NOT ENGAGE with him who has nothing 'to lose. It is to fight at a disadvantage, for the other enters without encumbrance, because unaccoutred even of shame; and having auctioned off everything, he has nothing more to lose, and so may allow himself every insolence; never expose to such great hazard your treasured reputation: what cost you years to attain, can go to perdition and there be lost in one unlucky moment what has cost much precious sweat. It makes the man of honor pause and consider what he has at stake, for while regarding his own good name, he looks at that of the other, and so becomes entangled only after great consideration, proceeding with such caution, that prudence is given time to recall, and put in safe-keeping a reputation: for not even victory can bring in as much as was risked when a good name was merely exposed to loss.

ঽ৬ 1 7 3 ঽ৬

NOT TOO FRAGILE in bumping up against the world and least so with your friends. Some crack with the greatest ease, showing that they are made of poor stuff; they fill themselves with imagined wrongs, and all others with vexation; they show their natures to be more soft, than the eyes themselves, so none may touch them, either in fun, or in earnest; such trifles bruise that real hurt is not necessary. They must watch their step who have dealings with them, alert always to their great sensitiveness, and on guard against every draft, since the slightest disturbance upsets them; these people are commonly selfish, the slaves of their whims, for which they would sacrifice everything, worshippers of their imagined honor; but the heart of friendship is like the heart of a diamond in its enduringness, and in its firmness.

ஃ 174 ஃ

D O NOT LIVE at too great pace. To know how to
spread out things, is to know how to enjoy them:
many have finished with their luck before they have
finished with their lives; they miss happiness because
they do not know how to enjoy; and so they would
afterwards turn back, for they have so quickly outrun
themselves; veritable positions of life, who to the general runaway add their own impatient whip. They seek
to swallow in a day, what can scarce be digested in a
lifetime; they live swiftly through every joy, eating up
the years to come, and as they crowd forward in such
haste, they are quickly through with everything; even
in the quest after knowledge it is well to have reserve,
in order not to learn those things which are better not
learned; the days of life are more than the joys thereof;
wherefore go slowly in enjoyment, but in work make
haste: for the day's labors are gladly finished, but not so
gladly, its joys.

ஃ 175 ஃ

A MAN OF SUBSTANCE, and he who is, has little
fondness for those who are not. Unhappy the
conspicuousness that does not rest upon a sure foundation. Not all who seem to be, are men, but fakes,
conceived as hybrids and born humbugs; many more

are like unto them, in that they bolster them, taking more delight in the false, which promises most, because most, than in the truth, which promises little, because so little. In the end their shams fare badly, for they lack foundation in truth, and only truth can bestow a true reputation, and only solid character prove profitable; one fraud makes necessary another and more; and so the whole of what is built up is flimsy, and as it rests upon air, it is destined to return to earth. Never has mere scenery lasted, for an outward show that promises too much, is sufficient to make itself suspect, just as that which is overly proved, is held impossible.

ἐς **1 7 6** ₰

K NOW, OR HEARKEN to him who knows. You cannot live without knowledge, either your own, or borrowed, but there be many who do not know that they know nothing, and others who think that they know, but know nothing; these deformities of the mind are incurable, whence it is that the ignorant neither know themselves nor yet how to gain what they lack: some would be wise, if they did not believe themselves wise, wherefore it comes to pass that the oracles of wisdom even though few, live neglected, because no one consults them; it does not dwarf grandeur, or argue against capacity to seek advice, yea, to seek advice, brings credit: better to reason it out than to fight it out with misfortune.

❧ 1 7 7 ❧

A VOID FAMILIARITIES IN the daily round.
Neither practice them yourself, nor permit them
to be practiced upon you. He who allows them, forfeits
at once that sovereignty, which his character merits,
and respect to boot: the stars do not get intimate with
us, but hold themselves aloof in their splendor, for the
divine demands respect, and everything too human
makes easy disrespect; earthly affairs even as they
become more human, become more cheap; because
through communion they communicate their tawdri-
ness, which distance concealed; it is well never to get
on common ground with anyone, not with your betters, because that is dangerous, and not with your infe-
riors, because that is indecent; least of all with the
common herd, for it is insolent because it is ignorant,
and failing to recognize the favor done it, presumes
upon it as a right; intimacy borders on vulgarity.

❧ 1 7 8 ❧

T RUST TO YOUR heart, especially when it is
being proved, for it is never untrue to itself, often
foretelling what is of greatest import; a veritable
inward oracle; many have died of what they feared: but
why did they fear without doing something about it?
Some have a heart most faithful, the advantage of a

great nature, which always forewarns them, and sounds the alarm in order that danger may be met; there is no sense in sallying forth looking for trouble; but if such sally be made, let it be to engage the enemy and overcome him.

֎ 1 7 9 ֎

R ESERVE IS THE seal of capacity: the breast without its hiding place, is an open letter: secrets are buried best where there is depth, for there lie caverns and bays where treasure may be hid; profundity is the product of a great mastery over self, and to be master in this, is to be a conqueror indeed; the heart must pay tribute, to all to whom it reveals itself; in inner quiet lies the salvation of the spirit; what threatens reserve are the attacks of others; as those of contradiction, in order to excite it; or those of baiting, in order to drive it from cover, which will only make the observant shut up more tightly. Those things which are to be done, should not be talked about, and those which have been talked about, should not be done.

֎ 1 8 0 ֎

N EVER BE MISLED by what your foe does. If a fool he will not do what a wiser thinks best, because he never knows what is best; and if a man of discretion, not then, because he wishes to cloak his intent, even to the point of forestalling the other; every situation must be looked at from two points of view and be considered first from one side, and then the other, to be disposed of from either angle; the minds of men differ greatly, wherefore let judgment remain alert, not so much because of what is happening, as because of what may.

1 8 1

WITHOUT LYING, DO not speak the whole truth; there is nothing that requires more careful handling than the truth, for it is a bleeding from the heart; just as necessary to know how to utter the truth, as to know how to hush it; a whole reputation for uprightness may be ruined with a single lie, for a lie is held treachery, and the liar a traitor, which is worse; not all truths may be spoken, because some matter to us, and some matter to others.

1 8 2

A BIT OF AUDACITY in everything is common sense. It is to step down your concept of the others in order not to believe them so exalted, that you fear them; never allow your imagination to make surrender to your heart; some appear great, until you meet them; but communion with them, serves more to bring disillusion to you than exaltation to them; none gets beyond the confines of the human; there is in every one a But; in some, of the heart, and in some of the spirit. Rank bestows the apparent superiority; but only rarely is it accompanied by personal qualification: for fate has a way of avenging greatness of office by meanness of the occupant; the imagination always hurries forward, and paints things brighter than they are: conceding not only what is, but what might be: let calm judgment, so often disillusioned be experience, correct the picture, in order that stupidity be not too bold, nor virtue too timorous; if self-confidence has at times availed the simpleton, of how much more use might it not be to the deserving, and to the understanding?

ༀ **1 8 3** ༀ

HOLD TO NOTHING too violently. Every fool stands convinced; and everyone convinced is a fool; and the faultier a man's judgment, the firmer his conviction; even with the proof on your side, it is well to make concession; for your reasons are known and your gentlemanliness is recognized; more is lost in contention than can be gained in consummation; for such does not defend the truth, but only exhibits bad manner; blockheads are difficult or impossible of conversion; for when conviction is joined to obstinacy, both are indissolubly married to stupidity. Inflexibility should lie in the will, and not in the judgment. Yet there be exceptions when you may not yield without danger of being twice conquered; first in your decision, and then in its execution.

ᓂ 1 8 4 ᓂ

DO NOT STAND on ceremony. For even in a king this affectation was celebrated as something ridiculous. Punctiliousness frets the spirit, and yet whole nations put on such show. The apparel of fools is patched of such pieces, idolaters of their self-importance, which they prove to be founded upon little, because constantly in fear that something will injure it; well to demand respect, but not so well to be considered a grand master of pomposity: yet it is the truth, that the man without all show must need be possessed of the greatest virtues; good form should not be affected, nor yet despised; but it does not evidence greatness to be a mere stickler about trifles.

ᓂ 1 8 5 ᓂ

NEVER RISK YOUR reputation on a single shot for if you miss, the loss is irreparable. It is very easy to go wrong once, and especially the first time: not always is this the right moment, wherefore it is said: wait for your day. Assure yourself therefore of a second chance through the first, if it went wrong, or if it went right, let the first have been the pawn for the second; always hold in reserve recourse to something better, and the reputation of having something more: everything depends upon circumstance, and very much so, whence it comes that the happiness is so rare of the happy ending.

≈ 186 ≈

KNOW WHAT IS evil, however much worshiped it may be. Let the man of intelligence not fail to recognize it, even if clothed in brocade, or crowned with gold, because it cannot thereby hide its bane; slavery does not lose its infamy, however noble the master; the vices may stand high, but they are not high: some see a great man afflicted with this vice or that; but they do not see, that he is great not because of it but in spite of it. The portrait of the man high up is so convincing, that even his deformities persuade, wherefore flattery at times mimics them, not seeing, that if in the great such things are overlooked, in the small, they are looked down upon.

❦ 1 8 7 ❦

A LL THAT GAINS approval, do yourself, and all
that gains disapproval through another. By the
first you invite affection, and by the second you avoid
hatred. More satisfying to the great to do good, than
to receive it, for it is the joy of the spirit: rarely can one
give pain to another without suffering it himself, either
through compassion, or through commiseration: God
himself does not work without reward, or without ret-
ribution; dealing out the good directly, and the bad
indirectly: wherefore keep at hand someone to absorb
the recoils of discontent, which are hatred, and abuse:
madness in a crowd is like madness in dogs, who failing
to recognize the cause of their suffering, turn upon
their muzzles which though not at fault, are made to
suffer as though they were.

❦ 1 8 8 ❦

T O BE THE bearer of good report, proves your
good taste, for it shows that you knew the best
elsewhere, and that you may be relied upon for correct
opinion on what is here: he who knew quality yesterday, will know it again today: to commend what is
praiseworthy, is to make for conversation, and for emu-
lation. It is the polite way of paying obeisance to the
perfect in those about you; others, on the contrary,
always choose to be the bearers of evil report, flatter-

ing those present by detraction of those absent; they come off well with the superficial, who do not recognize this trick of speaking evil of the one to the other; some have made politics of the matter of cherishing more the mediocrities of today, than the great of yesterday. Let the astute see through these cunnings of the bearer, and be not dismayed by the tall tales of the one, or inflated by the flattery of the other, realizing that behavior with the one group is as with the other, changing in mind and in action according to the spot at which the tale bearer has arrived.

ᷨ 1 8 9 ᷨ

K NOW HOW TO make use of another's want; for if it rises to the level of lust, it becomes the most effective of thumbscrews. The philosophers declare desire to be nothing, the politicians, everything. The latter are the wiser. They make of the desires of others the stepping stones to their own ends. They utilize the opportunity, and by emphasizing the difficulties of satisfying such desires, sharpen the appetite. For they are assured of more through the heat of passion, than through the lukewarmness of possession; for as resistance to what is wanted increases, desire grows: a very subtle way of accomplishing your own purposes, to keep men dependent upon you.

༇ 1 9 0 ༃

FIND CONSOLATION IN everything. Even the worthless live forever. There is no sorrow unmitigated, the fools finding it in their luck, which makes proverbial the luck of the hunchback. To live long, it is only necessary to be worth little; it is the cracked pot that is never broken, for which reason it irritates because it lasts so long: it is against those who really count that fortune holds her grudge, for she bestows length of days upon the bums and shortness of days upon those who are something. The greater their worth, the sooner they die, while those of no profit live forever, at times because they seem to, at others because they really do. To him in misery it looks as though fortune, and death, had both conspired to forget him.

༇ 1 9 1 ༃

DO NOT CONSIDER an account squared by mere excess of manner, for it is a species of fraud. In order to bewitch, some men need not the herbs of Thessaly, for they enchant fools with one airy wave of the hat, which makes them swoon. They make toadying a business, and pay their way with the wind of fine words. He who promises everything, promises nothing, and yet he who merely promises ensnares the fools; real manner is an obligation, but its affectation, a deception, especially if out of order: it is not decency then, but subserviency. All of which exhibits respect not for the person but for his goods, and pays compliment not to his talents which are apparent but to his profits which are hoped for.

ఙ 1 9 2 ಜ

A MAN OF peace, a man of years; in order to live, let live; the peaceful not only live, but they reign; lend your ears, and your eyes, but hold your tongue; the day without strife, makes the night with its sleep: to live long, and to live in joy, is to live twice, and the fruit of peace; he has everything who gives no concern to what does not concern him; nothing more purposeless, than to see purpose in everything, for it is equally stupid to break the heart over what is not your business, as not to set your teeth into that which is.

ఙ 1 9 3 ಜ

L OOK TO HIM who comes in with another's concern, in order to go out with his own. There is no defense against trickery like that of watchfulness; against a code, a good decoder: some make of the affairs of others, their own, and unless their purpose is recognized your every move will only get you deeper into the job of withdrawing from the fire the chestnuts of another, to the great damage of your own hand.

ༀ 1 9 4 ༀ

A PROPER CONCEIT of yourself, and of your aims, especially at the start of life. All have a high opinion of themselves, particularly those with least reason; each dreams himself a fortune, and imagines himself a prodigy: hope wildly promises everything, and time then fulfills nothing: these things torment the spirit, as the imagined gives way before the truth, wherefore let the man of judgment correct his blunders, and even though hoping for the best, always expect the worst, in order to be able to accept with equanimity whatever comes. It is well, of course, to aim somewhat high, in order to near the mark; but not so high that you miss altogether a starting upon your life's job; to make this proper estimate of yourself is absolutely necessary, for without experience it is very easy to confuse the conjectured with the fact; there is no greater panacea against all that is foolish, than understanding; wherefore let every man know what is the sphere of his abilities, and his place, and thus be able to make the picture of himself coincide with the actual.

ༀ 1 9 5 ༀ

K NOW HOW TO appraise. There is none, who cannot be the master of another in something; or having excelled, cannot be excelled: to know how to

pick the fruit from every man's tree is profitable knowledge; the wise man knows the value of everything
because he recognizes the good in everything, and
knows how much it takes to make things good. Only a
fool is scornful of everything, through ignorance of what
is good, and through bad choice of what is no good.

ᘓ *1 9 6* ᘔ

K NOW YOUR STAR. None is so forgotten that
he has none, and if yours be an unlucky one, it is
because you do not know your own. Some stand high
in the favor of princes, and of potentates, knowing not
why, or wherefore, but that their luck followed them;
to help it along they needed only industry; others discover themselves in the graces of the wise; some are
better received of one nation than another, or made
more welcome in this city, than in that; thus also is
more satisfaction to be gained in one position, or
place, than in another, even though in what they offer
they appear to be alike or actually are identical: fate
shuffles the cards as and when she chooses; let each
know his own star, as he knows his own mind, for it
determines whether he shall perish, or be saved; let
him know how to follow it, and keep pace with it,
never mistaking it, for that would be to miss the polar
star itself, to which the nearby Little Bear is constantly
pointing.

❧ 1 9 7 ❧

D O NOT SADDLE yourself with fools: he is one who does not know them, and a greater, he who knowing them, does not shake them off, for they are dangerous in the daily round, and deadly as confidants, even if at times their cowardice restrains them; or the watchful eye of another; in the end they commit some foolishness, or speak it, which if they tarry over it, is only to make it worse: slight aid to another's reputation, he who has none himself; they are full of woes, the welts of their follies, and they trade in the one for the other; but this about them is not so bad, that even though the wise are of no service to them, they are of much service to the wise, either as example, or as warning.

❧ 1 9 8 ❧

B E KNOWN AS transplantable. There are exotics, which in order to flower, need change of soil, and especially those most rare. The home country is a step-mother to its own great talent: jealousy rules her, as the land itself, and she remembers better the weakness in which a man started, than the strength to which he grew: a needle gains distinction when passed from one country into another, and glass makes diamonds look cheap when carried elsewhere; all that is foreign is cherished, at times because it comes from afar, at times because it arrives complete; and in its perfection: there be men who were once the despised of their circle, who today are the honored of the world, respected by their compatriots, and those foreign; by the one, because they are seen from a distance, and by the other because they come from a distance; never will he pay homage to the idol upon the altar, who knew it as a stump in the forest.

❦ 1 9 9 ❦

KNOW HOW TO make a place for yourself through desert, and not through push. The right road to distinction, is that of merit, and when industry is joined to worth, it is a short cut to the stars; but mere goodness is not enough, and push is unbecoming, for then things arrive so soiled, that they produce loathing; best is the middle course between merit, and a knowledge of how to usher yourself in.

❦ 2 0 0 ❦

LEAVE SOMETHING TO be desired, in order not through glut to become unhappy, for the body should want air, and the spirit have its longings: when all is yours, all turns to ashes, and disappoints, for even the mind must be left its passion to know, to pique its curiosity and to keep hope alive: a surfeit of happiness is fatal; in bestowing reward it is wisdom never to gratify: when nothing more is to be wished for, everything is to be feared, the most unfortunate of fortunes, for where desire ends, apprehension begins.

ఇ𝅃 **2 0 1** 𝅃ఇ

FOOLS ALL WHO seem it, and the half of those who do not. The world is filled of folly and if there be any wisdom in it, this is folly compared to that of heaven; but the greatest fool is he who does not know himself one, and declares all others such. For to be wise, it is not enough to seem it, least of all to yourself: he knows, who knows that he does not know; and does not see, who does not see that the others see: with the whole world full of fools, there is none who thinks himself one, or even suspects it.

ఇ𝅃 **2 0 2** 𝅃ఇ

WORDS, AND DEEDS make the consummate man. It is to voice what is good and to do what is honorable; the first evidences a good head, the second a good heart, and together they give birth to a great soul; words are the ghosts of deeds; the former are the ewes, the latter the rams; of greater moment to be cheered, than to be the cheer leader: to say something is easy, but to do something, difficult. Achievement is the substance of life, and praise, its decoration; greatness in action endures, greatness in words, passes, for deeds are the fruits of the mind, which when wise, makes triumphant.

❧ **2 0 3** ☙

RECOGNIZE THE GREAT of your period. They
will not be many; one Phoenix in all the world,
one great captain, one perfect orator, one sage in the
whole of a century, one illustrious king among the
many; it is the mediocrities that make up the crowd
both in number and in kind, for the great are few,
because they require the cloak of perfection; and the
higher their rating, the greater the difficulty of achiev-
ing the top; many have seized for themselves the sur-
name of great, from Caesar, or Alexander, but in vain,
for without deeds, the voice is not more than a bit of
air; few Senecas have had their habitation among us,
and fame celebrates but one Apelles.

❧ **2 0 4** ☙

APPROACH THE EASY as though it were difficult, and the difficult, as though it were easy; the
first, lest overconfidence make you careless, and the
second, lest faint-heartedness make you afraid; nothing
more is required in order to do nothing, than to think
it done; to go at the job, on the other hand, accomplishes the impossible; but the greatest undertakings
should not be overly pondered, lest contemplation of
difficulties too clearly foreseen appall you.

❧ 2 0 5 ❧

KNOW THE VALUE of disdain. A trick for the attainment of an end, to be contemptuous of it; the quarry which cannot be captured while pursued, commonly falls into our hands if we but halt: as all things temporal are but the shadows of the heavenly, they become ghostly in this also, that they flee from the pursuer, and pursue him who flees from them. Disdain, moreover, is the most politic form of vengeance; a rare maxim of the wise never to defend yourself with the pen, for it leaves a mark, that serves more to glorify the adversary, than to check his impudence; a trick of the worthless, to appear the adversaries of great men, in order indirectly to make themselves as celebrated, as directly they merit nothing. For many would never have been heard of, had their excellent opponents not paid heed to them. There is no revenge like unto that of forgetting, for it is to bury them in the dust of their own nothingness. These brash try to immortalize themselves, by setting fire to the wonders of the world, and the centuries; the way to silence slander is to ignore it; to fight against it, is to prejudice your own case; for even though you win you will still have lost and satisfaction goes to your adversary; for the slightest cloud can darken, even when it cannot obscure the whole of a great name.

⤖ 2 0 6 ⤖

OBSERVE THAT THE ordinary lies all about. Even in Corinth herself. Even in the best of families. And each may by himself discover it within the portals of his own house; but beyond the ordinary there flourishes the vulgar, which is worse; this specialty has all the properties of the familiar, as the fragments of a mirror have those of the unbroken, but more jagged; it talks like a fool, and impertinently finds fault; it is the great disciple of ignorance, the godfather of idiocy, and the defender of what is not so, for which reason no heed need be paid to what it says, and less to what it thinks, but it is important to know it, in order to get free of it, whether in man, or in object: for whatever smacks of folly is vulgar, and the vulgar are all fools.

⤖ 2 0 7 ⤖

USE SELF-RESTRAINT. Especially well to have considered the chance when a mischance. There are heats of passion in which the reason slides, wherein lies the danger of going to perdition. One second of rage, or one of stupid self-satisfaction, brings more in its wake than many hours of listlessness. They occasion in a moment, what to correct afterwards requires a lifetime. The craftiness of another may thus try to tempt your soul, to discover where you stand, or what you think: using it like a thumbscrew upon your inner self, to drive mad the best of minds. Match such wiliness by your self-restraint, particularly in fast repartee; great control is necessary if passion is not to break the bit, for a great head has he who has such a horse; he goes with caution who knows the danger; light as seems a word to him who tosses it off, even so heavy may it seem to him who catches it, and weighs it.

৵ **2 0 8** ৵

DO NOT DIE of the fool's sickness. The wise usually perish of mental starvation; and the fools, of the mental glut of too much counsel. To die like a fool, is to die of too much thinking; some die because they have sense, and others live because they have none; thus both are fools, the latter because they do not die of grief, and the former because they do. A fool is one who dies of too much brain: from which it comes that some die of reason and others live for no reason; but with many dying because fools, few fools die.

৵ **2 0 9** ৵

TO KEEP FREE from the popular inanities, marks especially good sense. They are highly esteemed because so well introduced; and many a man who could not be trapped by some particular stupidity, could not escape the general; one vulgar opinion holds that none is content in his fortune even though the best, and that none is discontented with his mind, even though the worst. Another, that all are covetous and look with unhappiness upon what is their own, and with joy upon what is another's. Again, that they of today glorify only the things of yesterday, and those from here only the things from afar. Or that all that is past is better, and everything that is distant, more valuable. As great a fool he who laughs at everything, as he who weeps over everything.

ক্ষ **2 1 0** ক্ষ

K NOW HOW TO deal out the truth. She is dangerous, and yet the upright man cannot escape speaking her: here is where art is required; the skilled physicians of the soul have devised a method of sweetening her, for when she is about to act upon error, she is the quintessence of bitterness. Avail yourself here of the nimbleness of good form, for the selfsame truth that wheedles one, cudgels another; be able to speak of things present in the terms of things past. With him who can understand, a hint is sufficient; but where nothing is sufficient, there go dumb. Princes may not be cured with remedies bitter, wherefore it becomes an art to know how to gild the naked truth.

❧ 2 1 1 ❧

IN HEAVEN ALL is gladness. In hell all is sorrow. Upon this earth, since it lies between, sometimes the one, and sometimes the other. We have our being between the two extremes, and so it partakes of both. Fortune should vary, not all being felicity, nor all adversity. This world is a zero, and by itself worth nothing, but joined to heaven worth everything: indifference to your lot is common sense, and not to be surprised by it, wisdom. Our life becomes more complicated as we go along, like a comedy, but toward its end it becomes simpler; keep in mind, therefore, the happy ending.

❧ 2 1 2 ❧

KEEP THE ULTIMATE refinements of your art to yourself. This is the law of the great masters who must themselves employ best the subtilties of their art even as they teach them, for only thereby do they remain on top and so the masters: art must be put into the teaching of art, lest its source and its capacity be forgotten; only thus can you maintain your reputation, and the dependence of others upon you. In the business of pleasing and instructing others, this is good advice, feed their wonder, and satisfy their anticipation: to have a reserve in everything is the great law to life and to conquest, especially in those occupations most exalted.

ᖷ **2 1 3** ᖷ

KNOW HOW TO debate. It is the craft of explo-
ration intended not to entangle you but to entangle the other. It is a unique form of torture to make the
feelings flinch; luke-warmness in believing is a true
emetic of the secrets of the heart, a key to the tightest
of locked breasts, making possible a most sensitive
probing, both of the mind, and of the intent; a cautious
questioning of the vagaries uttered by another, ferrets
out the most hidden secrets, drives them into the
mouth to be chewed over, until they fall from the
tongue, to be caught in the snare of your artifice;
reserve on your part, makes the other throw it to the
winds, whereby his feelings are exposed, even though
by any other method his heart would have been
closed. The affectation of doubt, is the nimblest lock-
pick that curiosity can employ, in order to discover
whatever it seeks or even, what it would learn; a good
trick on the part of the pupil to bait his teacher, who
thereby excites himself to greater effort in the declara-
tion, and the foundation of his beliefs; whence it
comes that well-moderated debate makes for most
effective teaching.

❧ 2 1 4 ❧

BECAUSE AN ASS once, not twice. All too commonly in order to repair one foolish step, four
more are taken; or excuse is made for one dumb trick
with a second, and a greater; folly is either of the house
of lies, or lies are of the house of folly, for in order to
stand, each needs the support of many; worse than the
defense of evil, is its protection, and even worse than
the evil, the inability to hide it; the bequest of one
vice, is the bestowal of many others at interest: the wisest of men may slip once, but not twice, and that only
by chance, and not by design.

❧ 2 1 5 ❧

WATCH HIM WHO works by indirection. A
trick of the agent to put the will off guard that
he may steal upon it, for he who is outwitted is out-
done; such men conceal their intent only to attain it,
and put it in the background in order that when they
act it will be in the foreground, a shot that reaches its
mark through its very carelessness. But attention
should not be asleep, when intent is so awake, and
when this exits in order to deceive, let the other enter,
in order to undeceive; let caution note the craftiness
with which the man approaches, and recognize the
pretexts advanced to arrive at his purpose: one thing is

intended, another is pretended, and both are then skill-fully turned about to hit the very bull's-eye of his design; know therefore what you are conceding him, and perchance allow him to understand, that you understand.

ৰ্জ **2 1 6** ৰ্জ

B E ABLE TO express yourself, not only clearly, but with charm. Some conceive easily, but have a hard delivery; yet without pains these children of the spirit, our thoughts and our judgments, are not rightly born; others are like those vessels which hold much but yield little; while conversely others pour forth more than was anticipated; what resolution is to the will, exposition is to the mind, and both are great attributes; clear heads are much praised, but those balmy may be venerated because not understood; wherefore at times be not too clear, in order not to seem too ordinary; yet how can a world get a concept of what it hears, if the speaker himself has no clear notion of what he is talking about?

ৰ্জ **2 1 7** ৰ্জ

N EITHER LOVE, NOR hate without end. Confide in the friends of today, as though the enemies of tomorrow, and the worst; and because such things come to pass, be prepared; do not provide the deserters of friendship with the arms, by which to make better war; toward your enemies on the other hand, keep open a door of reconciliation, and let it be a wide one, for that is safest: the thirst for vengeance yesterday becomes the torment of today, and the joy in revenge past, resolves into the remorse present.

ঞ্জ *2 1 8* ঝ

NEVER ACT THROUGH obstinacy, but only through reason. Every obstinacy is a boil, the pussy daughter of passion, she who has never yet done anything right: there are those who reduce everything to war, veritable highwaymen of friendly intercourse; they seek that all they push through be made a victory; and they know not peaceful pursuit. For command, or for rule, such men are pernicious, for they make edict of law, and foes of those who should be made their friends: they would arrange for their ends by intrigue, and attain them as the fruit of their craftiness; but when the great mass has dragged their duplicity into the open, it rises against them; it thwarts their plans and so they accomplish nothing; they go away o'erladen with trouble, and everyone adds to their burden. These men have crooked minds, and often accursèd hearts: the way to treat these misbegotten, is to flee from them even to the Antipodes, for its crudeness is more tolerable, than their savageries.

ఇ**2 1 9**ఇ

D O NOT BE held a cheat, even though it is impossible to live today without being one. Better prudent, than crafty: to be smooth in your way is to please everybody, but not everybody of your own house. Do not let your sincerity degenerate into simple-mindedness, nor your intelligence into trickery. Better be esteemed for your wisdom, than feared for your foxiness; the simple in heart are loved, even though they are cheated. Let your greatest cunning lie in covering up what looks like cunning. In the golden age it was simplicity that flourished; in this, the iron age, it is duplicity. To have the name of a man who knows what should be done, is honorable, and inspires trust, but to have that of being a sham, is disreputable, and engenders mistrust.

ఇ**2 2 0**ఇ

W HEN UNABLE TO wear the lion's skin, clothe yourself in the fox's. To know how to yield to the times, is to be ahead of them: he who accomplishes his purpose, never endangers his reputation; where force fails, try art; over one road, or another, either the highway of courage, or the byway of cunning: more things have been gained by knack, than by knock, and the wise have won much oftener than the valorous, and not the other way about; when not possible to attain your end, register your contempt for it.

ৰু **2 2 1** ৯ৎ

DO NOT BE a source of embarrassment either to yourself, or to others. There be men who offend the decencies, as much their own, as those of others, and always foolishly; they are met with easily, and parted from with difficulty; no day complete for them without its hundred annoyances; they have a humor for nothing, and so they gainsay everybody, and everything: they put on their understanding wrong side to, and so find fault with everything. But the greatest traducers of the mind are those, who unable to do anything right themselves, call the efforts of all others wrong. Which explains why so many beasts roam the broad fields of the wild.

ৰু **2 2 2** ৯ৎ

A MAN SELF-CONTROLLED, for it evidences prudence. The tongue is a beast, which once at large, is hard to recapture and to chain: it is the pulse of the soul, from which the trained deduce its state; here the man observant feels the beat of the spirit: a sad fact that he who should be most restrained, is often least so; a wiser man does not get himself stirred up or involved thereby proving how much he is the master of himself. He goes carefully, a Janus in outlook, an Argus in discernment. It would have been better if Momus had cried for eyes in the hands instead of that little window in the breast.

≈ **2 2 3** ≈

NOT TOO INDIVIDUAL, either by affectation, or through carelessness: some individualize themselves by the craziness of their actions, but such had better be regarded as disgraces, than as distinctions; just as some stand forth because of ugly face, these become known by the excrescences upon their deportment. But these matters do not serve to make the individual, but only to mark him, and in very special fashion, for they merely move men, at times to laughter, and at times to tears.

≈ **2 2 4** ≈

KNOW HOW TO take things, never against the grain, even though they come that way. Everything has its cutting, and its blunt edge; the best and most useful of tools, if seized by the blade, wounds; while, on the contrary, the most destructive if grasped by the hilt, protects: much that has given pain, if it had been taken rightly, would have given pleasure;

for there is pleasure, or pain in everything, and wisdom lies in hitting upon the profitable; for one and the same thing has very different faces, as seen in different lights; look upon it in its happiest light; and do not get the controls mixed, as to what is good and what is bad: from this it comes that some discover satisfaction in everything, and others only grief: the great defense against the reverses of fortune, and a master rule of life, at all times and in all circumstances.

ᎈ **2 2 5** ᎋ

K NOW YOUR CHIEF weakness. No one lives without some counterweight even to his greatest gift, which when petted, assumes tyranny; start war upon it, by calling out caution, and let your first move be a manifesto against it, for as soon as recognized, it may be conquered, especially if the victim sees as clearly, as the onlookers; to be master of yourself, you must rise above yourself; bring this chief of your defects into subjection, and you finish off all the rest.

ᎈ **2 2 6** ᎋ

B E CIVIL. Most men neither speak nor act for what they are, but as they must; to persuade one of evil anything will do, because slander is easily believed, however unbelievable; the most and the best of what is ours resides in the opinion of others: some rest content because right is on their side; but this is not enough, for it needs the help of good form. To be obliging usually costs but little; yet it is worth much, for with mere words, you buy deeds; and there is no bauble so mean in this great house of the world, that once in the year it may not prove necessary, and however little its value, be missed if absent; every man regards a subject as it affects him.

✺ **2 2 7** ✺

NOT THE VICTIM of first impressions. Some men marry themselves to the first tale told, whence it follows that all others can only appear as concubines, and since the lie always pushes itself out in front no room is left for the truth; but neither our wish for the first seen, nor our sympathy for the first heard, should thus be able to stuff us, for that marks a lack of capacity; some men are like new casks which forever retain the smell of the first liquor poured into them, be it bad, or good. When this shortsightedness comes to be known, it is fatal, for it makes room for malicious gossip, allowing those of evil intent to tinge the credulous with their color, wherefore leave room always for a second impression; Alexander ever kept the other ear for the other side: save space for the second, and even the third report, for it argues small capacity to be too readily filled, and borders on the too passionate.

ᎧᎦ **2 2 8** ᎧᎦ

D O NOT BE a scandal sheet. Much less, be held one, for it is to have the reputation of being a reputation killer; do not be smart at the expense of another, which is more odious, than difficult; all take vengeance upon such a one, by speaking ill of him, and since he stands alone, and they are many, he is conquered more quickly, than they are convinced; evil should never be our pleasure, and therefore not our theme: the slanderer is forever despised, and even when, at times, great men are seen in his company, it is more because his mockery amuses them, than because his wisdom enchants them; and he who speaks evil will always have to hear still greater.

ᎧᎦ **2 2 9** ᎧᎦ

K NOW HOW TO arrange your life, with intelligence, and not as accident may determine, but with foresight, and choice. It is a toilsome affair without recreation, like a long journey without inns; variety in mental equipment makes it happier. Spend the first period of beautiful life, in conversation with the dead; we are born to know the world, and to know ourselves, and the great books of truth make us men. Let the second be spent with the living, to see, and to know all the good that is upon this earth, for not everything is found in one country; the omnipresent Father has divided His blessings and has, at times, adorned the ugliest in the richest raiment. Let the third be wholly your own, for to live in the mind is the ultimate good fortune of man.

༔ 2 3 0 ༔

OPEN YOUR EYES betimes: not all who see, see with open eyes, and not all who look, see. To see too late, brings not help, but grief; some start seeing when there is no longer anything to see, having sold off their house and substance before they ever came into them. A difficult matter, to put understanding into him who has no will, and more difficult to put will into him who has no understanding; those who comprehend play around such men as if they were blind, to everybody's amusement, and because they are deaf of ear, they do not open their eyes to see; but there is no lack of men to encourage this blindness, for they live because the others do not; an unhappy nag, whose master has no eyes: she will run badly to fat.

༔ 2 3 1 ༔

NEVER EXHIBIT YOUR things half-done, for they can be enjoyed only when complete. All beginnings are without form, and the image of this shapelessness tarries in the imagination; the memory of the thing seen imperfect lingers into the completed, forbidding the enjoyment of the magnificent in one gaze; even though this blurs the judgment of details, only through it is desire satisfied; before an object is everything, it is nothing, and in beginning to be, it is still very close to being nothing: the sight of preparation of even the daintiest morsel excites more to disgust, than to appetite; wherefore, let every great master look to it that his work be not seen in embryo, learning from nature herself not to bring it forth, until it is ready to be seen.

⁂ 2 3 2 ⁂

HAVE JUST A touch of the commercial in you. Do not merely shop, but trade a little. Most philosophers are easy to cheat, for even though they know the unusual, they are ignorant of the usual of life, which is much more necessary; the contemplation of affairs sublime leaves them no time for thought of affairs mundane; and as they do not know the first thing about that which they ought to know, and about which all others can split hairs, they are either marveled at, or considered fools by the ignorant of the common herd; wherefore, let the man of wisdom see to it that he has a little of the commercial in him, just enough to keep him from being cheated, or even, from being laughed at; let him be a man fitted to the daily round, for even if this is not the highest thing in life, it is the most necessary: of what use is knowledge, unless it be made to function? And to know how to live today is the truest of sciences.

ॐ **2 3 3** ॐ

DO NOT FAIL to catch the other's mood; lest you give him pain instead of pleasure. With that by which some would oblige, they molest, because they do not grasp the spirit; ways that flatter one, offend another, and what was intended as a compliment, becomes an affront: it has often cost more to make a man unhappy, than it would have cost to make him happy: and so his gratitude and his thanks are lost, because the guiding star to his pleasure was not seen, for when you do not sense another's mood, it is hard to bring him satisfaction: whence it comes that many in trying to voice a eulogy, have pronounced a curse, and thus brought upon themselves a well-merited punishment; others think to charm by their eloquence, when they only bruise the spirit by their loquacity.

ॐ **2 3 4** ॐ

NEVER TRUST YOUR honor to another without the pawn to his. Proceed so that the advantage of silence or the danger of breaking it, is mutual. In matters of honor the interests of the whole company must always be at stake; whence it comes that the name of one is guarded by each of the rest. Never trust your honor to another; but if you should at some time let it be with all that art, which is demanded when intelligence makes concession to caution. Let the risk be mutual, and the need reciprocal, so that he who knows himself an accomplice will not convert himself into a witness against you.

✥ **2 3 5** ✥

KNOW HOW TO beg. Nothing more difficult for some, and nothing easier for others. There are those who do not know how to refuse and with such it is not necessary to be a burglar. There be others to whom the No is always the first word and at any hour; with these art is necessary, and with everybody, the right moment: catch them in a happy mood, when recently refreshed in body, or spirit: and when the attention of the patron has not already been awakened and has not foreseen the trick of the supplicant: the days of joy are the days in which favors are conferred, for they flow from the inside upon the outside. Do not approach, when another has just been turned away, for at that moment all fear of saying No is gone. And after affliction is not a good time: previously to have placed the other under obligation to you, is to make the transaction merely a trade, provided, of course, that you are not dealing with a villain.

༄ 2 3 6 ༅

FIRST MAKE AN obligation, of what you are paid for afterwards; it is a trick of the political giants, to yield favor before it is earned, for it betokens that the men concerned are men of honor. The favor thus advanced, has double merit, for in the readiness with which it was bestowed, it lays greater obligation upon him who receives it, and if later it is mere pay, given earlier, it constitutes a promissory note. This is a subtle way of evening obligations, for what the one must do to discharge his debt, the other must do to discharge his duty. But this is true only between men with a sense of honor, for to mean-minded men, advance payment of a pledge acts more as a rein, than as a spur.

༄ 2 3 7 ༅

NEVER PARTICIPATE IN the secrets of those above you: you think to share the fruit, and you share the stones: wherefore so many confidants die of want: they are bread sops, and run the risk of being eaten afterwards: the confidence of a prince is not a grant, but a tax. Many have broken the mirror, that reminded them of their ugliness, and so we do not truly wish to see him who has seen us truly; nor will we welcome him, to whom we are unwelcome. Hold a whip hand too heavily over no one, least of all over the man in power; letting this be for favors bestowed, rather than for favors received, for the confidences of friendship are dangerous above all other things on earth. He who tells his secrets to another, makes himself his slave, and this is a strain upon those who rule that cannot last: they will wish to regain their lost freedom, and to do so will trample upon everything, even justice; secrets, therefore, should never be heard, and never spoken.

ॐ 2 3 8 ॐ

KNOW THE CHINK in your armor. Many would count as great persons, were it not that they lack something, without which they can never attain the heights of being; it is obvious that many might be something much, if they could repair something little; thus certain men lack earnestness, which blurs their great gifts, and others lack friendliness of disposition, a fault which those about them note all too quickly, especially in men of position; some want execution, and others, temper: all such frailties, if they were given heed, could easily be overcome, for a little care is able to impose upon the inborn a second nature.

ॐ 2 3 9 ॐ

NOT TOO SMART, for it is more important to be wise; to display too much edge is to go dull, for what is too pointed commonly breaks off: most secure is the ordained truth; well to have fine brains, but not a babbling tongue; for too much discourse, borders on dispute; best is a good level judgment, that does not wander afield more than may be necessary.

ᚙ **2 4 0** ᚙ

K NOW HOW TO pretend ignorance. The wisest of men may at times play this part, for there are many occasions, when the better wisdom consists in showing that you have none; do not be ignorant, but deport yourself as though ignorant; of little importance to be intelligent with the ignoramuses, or to have a mind among the witless; wherefore be able to speak to every man in his own language; he is not the fool who affects foolishness, but he who is affected of it; he is the simpleton, who cannot double in the part, for to this extremity has trickery driven us; in order to be welcome, the only way is to come clothed in the skin of the simplest of the brutes.

ᚙ **2 4 1** ᚙ

J OKES! Know how to take them, but do not play them: the first is a kind of gallantry; the second a way into difficulty; he who grows ill-humored at the fiesta, has much of a beast in him, and shows himself a greater; a good joke enlivens, and to know how to take it shows good head: let him who is piqued show no irritation toward him who piqued him, better yet, take no notice, and safest of all, to let it pass: for what is most serious has always sprung from what was most silly; there is nothing that demands greater caution, and greater skill; before you begin, know exactly to what point of sufferance the soul of your subject may be driven.

᧬ **2 4 2** ᧬

PURSUE YOUR ADVANTAGE. Some spend everything in getting started, and so never get anywhere: they plan but they do not build; the mark of a vacillating spirit, never to become distinguished, because nothing is followed through, but everything is left to itself, even when well conceived; in others it is the mark of impatience of the spirit, a failing of the Spaniards, just as patience is the virtue of the Belgians; they finish things, as the others are finished by them; some sweat to conquer a difficulty, only to rest content in their labors; not knowing how to bring victory home, which proves that they can but that they do not care; but this is really only evidence of incapacity, or of frivolousness; if the undertaking was good, why was it not finished? or if bad, why was it begun? let sagacity retrieve its prey, and not be content only to drive it from cover.

ༀ **243** ༀ

NOT ALWAYS THE innocent, but let the subtilty of the snake alternate with the simplicity of the dove. Nobody is easier to cheat than an honest man. He who never lies believes readily, and he who never cheats trusts readily. To be cheated does not always evidence stupidity, but often goodness: two kinds of men know well how to avoid hurt, the experienced, at their great cost; and the crafty, at the great cost of others. Here let intelligence show itself as able to disentangle, as craftiness is able to entangle, and let no one seek to be a man so honest, that he gives opportunity to the other to be dishonest; let him be a cross of the dove, with the snake, not a monster, but a marvel.

ༀ **244** ༀ

KNOW HOW TO engender obligation. Some can make a favor received look like a favor bestowed and it appears, or they make it appear, that they made payment, when they received it: there be men so ingenious, that they can turn what is to their advantage into what looks like opportunity for the other; by such trick they turn matters about, so that it seems as though the other had been done a service when actually he gave it, managing with extravagant politeness to reverse the order of the obligation, or at least making it doubtful who gained the profit from whom, having bought at the price of fine words the better bargain; through their exhibition of pleasure in something, they create also a sense of thankfulness, and satisfaction: they invoke courtesy to make an indebtedness out of what was given them; by this trick they change an obligation passive into the active, thus proving themselves better politicians, than grammarians; a great game this but a greater that of understanding it, reversing the nonsense, by restoring to each the honor due him, and by recovering for everyone what is rightfully his.

ᨠ **2 4 5** ᨠ

TALK ALWAYS ABOUT the uncommon, and forego the common, for it makes the better head; do not hold in too high opinion the man who never opposes you, for that is not a token of love for you, but of love for himself: do not allow yourself to be deceived through flattery, or be pleased by it, but cast it from you; always hold it to your credit that some men speak against you, especially if it be those who speak ill of all that is best; let that man pity himself whose ways please everybody, for it is a sign that they are of no value, for the excellent is of the few.

❧ 2 4 6 ❧

NEVER MAKE EXPLANATION unless asked, and even when asked, it is a species of crime, if over-done: to excuse yourself before occasion demands, is to accuse yourself; and to allow yourself to be bled in health, is to make eyes at disease, and at malice; to explain in advance is to awaken slumbering doubt; a man of sense will never show notice of another's suspicion, for that is to go hunting for trouble; then is the time to give it the lie through what is the uprightness of your whole way of life.

❧ 2 4 7 ❧

ENJOY A LITTLE more, and strive a little less: others argue to the contrary; but happy leisure is worth more than drive, for nothing belongs to us, except time, wherein even he dwells who has no habitation: equally infelicitous to squander precious existence in stupid drudgery, as in an excess of noble business. Be not crushed under success, in order not to be crushed under envy: it is to trample upon life, and to suffocate the spirit; some would include hereunder knowledge, but he who is without knowledge, is without life.

೫ **2 4 8** ಜ

DO NOT LET the latest carry you away. Some men forever hear the final news, which makes them go to ridiculous extremes, for they are as soft and as impressionable as wax, and therefore always carry the seal of the last signet, which has already stamped all the preceding: such men never stay put, because so mobile, every man tinting them with his own color; they are bad as confidants, children all their lives, and like them ever changing in spirit, and feelings, perpetually in a state of flux, and, always halt in will and in judgment, they wobble first to the one side, and then to the other.

೫ **2 4 9** ಜ

DO NOT START life wherewith it should be ended. Some take to rest at its beginning, and leave labor for its end; the essential should be first, and then, if chance is left, the accessory; others seek to triumph before they have battled, and some begin by study of the trivial, postponing those studies which might bring them fame and success, until the evening of life; another has not yet begun to climb toward fortune, when he goes dizzy; a knowledge of values is all-important, in order to learn, and be able to live.

༂ 2 5 0 ༄

WHEN MUST THE opposite be inferred? Whenever we are addressed by malice; with some everything must be turned about, for their Yes means No, and their No means Yes; when they decry anything, they have a high regard for it, for he who would gain something for himself, will cheapen it before others. Not all praise is meant well, for some in order not to praise the good, praise the evil, and to him to whom nothing is bad, nothing will be good, either.

༂ 2 5 1 ༄

EMPLOY HUMAN MEANS, as though there were no divine, and divine means, as though there were no human; these are the rules of the Great Master, and to them no comment need be added.

༂ 2 5 2 ༄

NEITHER WHOLLY YOURS, nor wholly another's: each is a vulgar tyranny. From wishing everything to himself, it follows that man must shortly want the whole world for himself; men of this stripe do not know how to yield the smallest point, or how to sacrifice an atom of their profit: they feel no obligation, trust to luck, and this support commonly fails them:

well at times to be dependent upon others, that the others may be dependent upon you; he who holds a public office, must be a public slave, else let him renounce his crown with his cargo, as said the old lady to Hadrian. On the other side stand those who belong too completely to others, for stupidity always goes to extremes, and in this instance most unhappily, for not a day, not even an hour remains their own, bound over so entirely, that one such has been called the man for everybody: this extends even unto their attitude, for they think only of everybody, and never of themselves; let the man of sense realize that none is looking out for him, but only has selfish interest in him, or through him.

❧ 2 5 3 ❧

A BIT VAGUE. For most men have low regard for what they understand, and venerate only what is beyond them: the things that they treasure must have cost them something, wherefore they honor most what they cannot grasp: always appear a little wiser, and smarter, than may be demanded by him with whom you deal, to command his respect, but properly, and not excessively; even though it be true that with men of understanding, wisdom counts for everything: for the majority some kind of oratory is still necessary, in order not to give them time for criticism, by keeping them busy with the mere business of interpretation:

many praise, but if asked can give no reason: Why? for they revere all that is hidden because mysterious, and they sing its praises, because they hear its praises sung.

ॐ 254 ॐ

DO NOT SCORN an evil though small, for it never comes singly, but in battalions, as does joy; good fortune and bad, concentrate where they are already thick, and it is the rule that all men flee the unfortunate, and tie up with the fortunate, for even the doves, with all their simplicity bow in homage to their most white. Everything fails the unlucky, himself, his reason, and his guiding star. Never awaken misfortune, when she sleeps; a slip is little, but to have this followed by a fall is fatal, for you do not know how far that will carry you; just as nothing that is good seems ever to come to fulfillment, so nothing that is bad seems ever to come to end. Against that which is sent us from heaven, patience, against that which springs from this earth, intelligence.

ॐ 255 ॐ

KNOW HOW TO do good, a little at a time, but often: never allow the obligation to exceed what can be repaid; for he who grants too much, no longer grants, but sells. Neither must the well of gratefulness be drained, for when it is seen that a quid pro quo is impossible, a friendship is done. Nothing more is necessary to lose most friends, than to place them in too heavy debt, for in order not to pay, they take themselves off, and from vassals turn into enemies. The idol does not care to be faced by the sculptor, who made it, nor the debtor have his benefactor before his eyes. Clever in giving, to bestow what costs little, but is wanted much, that it be cherished more.

੭ 2 5 6 ੭

GO PREPARED, ALWAYS, against the discourteous, the stubborn, the presumptuous, and every manner of fool. You encounter many, and intelligence lies in encountering none of them. Arm yourself daily with resolution on this point, before the mirror of your watchfulness, and thus be provided against foolish accident; go ready for the unexpected, never exposing public estimate of you to mere contingency: the man forearmed with intelligence, will not be engaged by impertinence. The way is difficult through this human sea, for it is filled with rocks upon which standing founders. To sail around them is safest, if counsel in seamanship be taken from Ulysses. Of great value in all these matters is a feigned blindness; cover everything with the cloak of courtesy, for that is the quiet way out of all embarrassments.

✿ 2 5 7 ✿

NEVER ARRIVE AT open rupture, for that is to come off with a wounded reputation. Every man counts as an enemy, but not every man as a friend. Very few can do us good, but nearly all, harm. The eagle no longer dwells securely even in the lap of Jupiter, from the day he has broken with a beetle. Hypocrites with open claw stir up the fire against you which has been smoldering in the hope of this opportunity: and from friends now spoiled, there emerge the worst of enemies. Each charges the other with faults that are his own, while of those who look on, each speaks as he feels, and feels as he wishes to feel: but all pronounce you guilty, because in the beginning you lacked prudence, in the end, patience, and at all times common sense; when a parting of the ways must come, find an excuse for it: and let it be rather a growing coolness between friends, than a mounting fury between enemies; here fits that saw about the well-ordered retreat.

✿ 2 5 8 ✿

DISCOVER SOMEONE TO help shoulder your misfortunes. Then you will never be alone, and even in the hour of danger, not freighted with all the distress; some think to carry off all the applause, and end by carrying off all the hisses: in such circumstance have at hand a confidant to make excuse for you, or to aid you in bearing the evil: neither fate, nor the crowd, so readily attacks two, which explains why the intelligent physician, having missed the cure, does not miss calling another, who under the name of consultant, helps him carry the coffin; divide with another your burdens, and your sorrows, for misfortune is doubly unbearable, to him who stands alone.

ᎦᏍ 2 5 9 ᎤᏍ

FORESEE INSULT, AND make of it, compliment, for it is cleverer to avoid insult, than to avenge it. It is a great trick to make a friend of him who wished to be a rival: and to turn into a protector of your honor, him who threatened its injury; it helps to know how to place him under obligation; time for insult is taken from him, who must fill it with thanksgiving, and it is to know how to live to be able to convert into pleasure, what was to have been pain: transform into trust, malevolence itself.

ᎦᏍ 2 6 0 ᎤᏍ

NEITHER BE ALL, nor give all to anyone: neither blood, nor friendship, nor the most pressing obligation, justifies it, for there is a big difference between the bestowal of your affection and the bestowal of yourself: the closest of ties must still admit of exceptions, and not on this account give offence to the laws of intimacy, for something should always be kept hidden even from a friend, and something concealed even from a father by his son: certain secrets are kept from the one and imparted to the other, and vice versa, wherefore it may be said that everything is revealed, or that everything is concealed, depending upon whom one is with.

੨ॐ **2 6 1** ॐ

DO NOT PERSIST in folly. Some make a duty of failure and having started down the wrong road, think it a badge of character to continue; they accuse themselves of error before the bar of their inner selves but before the bar of the outer world they excuse themselves, to the end that if at the start of their unwisdom they were marked imprudent, in its prosecution they are marked fools; neither rash promise, nor wrong resolve lays obligation upon any man; and yet some will on this account continue in their sulkiness, and carry on in their contrariness, wishing to be known as constant in their idiocies.

੨ॐ **2 6 2** ॐ

KNOW HOW TO forget, even though it's more luck than art. Matters best forgotten, are those best remembered, for memory plays the villain by forsaking us when we need her most, and the clown, by appearing when we would see her least; in all that gives pain she is most lavish, and in all that might give joy, most niggardly; at times the only remedy for an evil lies in forgetting it, and to be able to forget is the remedy; wherefore, train your memory to these comfortable manners, for she can bring you heaven, or hell: those self-satisfied are of course excepted, for in their state of innocence, they are already rejoicing in the happy state of feeble-mindedness.

?⁊ 2 6 3 ⁊₷

MANY OF THE things that bring delight should not be owned. They are more enjoyed if another's, than if yours; the first day they give pleasure to the owner, but in all the rest to the others: what belongs to another rejoices doubly, because without the risk of going stale, and with the satisfaction of freshness; everything tastes better after fasting, even the drink from another being judged nectar; the possession of things, not only diminishes their enjoyment, but augments their annoyance, whether shared, or not shared, for they are only held in stewardship and attract many more as enemies than as friends.

৫ষ **2 6 4** ৯ঌ

NO DAYS UNALERT; fate likes to play the buffoon, and to upset everything unawares in order to catch the sleeping; always stand ready for inspection in spirit, in mind, in fortitude, even in appearance, for the day that these are left to themselves becomes the day of their downfall; alertness when most necessary, is always missing, and not to give the matter a thought is to be slated for destruction; it has always been the strategy of another's watchfulness to call out your qualifications for most rigorous inspection, when in undress. The days for the parade are already known and may be discounted; but on the day least expected, she orders them up for review to test their real worth.

৫ষ **2 6 5** ৯ঌ

KNOW HOW TO put fire into your subordinates. The need to act, upon occasion, has made giants of many, just as the danger of drowning has made swimmers; under such circumstances many have discovered a courage, and even a capacity, which would have remained buried in their faint-heartedness, if the emergency had not offered: in danger lies the opportunity for fame, wherefore a nobleman who sees his honor threatened, has the energy of a thousand. Queen Isabela the Catholic knew and knew well, this law, as she knew all the others, of laying responsibility upon her subjects, and it was to such politic favor that the Great Captain owed his name, and many others their eternal glory; men are made great through such challenge.

༈ **2 6 6** ༈

DO NOT BECOME insipid by being too sweet: for such is he who never becomes outraged: men so insentient are hardly men; not always is this born of laziness, but of incapacity: proper feeling upon occasion, marks the man, for the birds soon amuse themselves of a scarecrow. To let the acrid alternate with the sweet, is proof of good taste; the sweet alone is for children, and fools; it is a grave disease, to be reduced through pure goodness to this state of feeling nothing.

༈ **2 6 7** ༈

SOFT WORDS, WITH tenderness of heart, for thorns pierce the body, but hard words, the spirit; a good cake gives good odor to the breath; a great trick in life to know how to sell the air; most things are paid for in words, and they suffice to discharge the impossible debt: heavenly business is done with the heavens and life-giving words give life: always carry the mouth full of sugar to sweeten the speech, that it may be found good even to your enemies: for the only way to be loved is to be amiable.

❧ 2 6 8 ❧

A WISE MAN does at once, what a fool does at last.
Both do the same thing; only at different times,
the first in season, and the second out. He who starts
by putting on his understanding wrong side to, must
continue in this style ever afterwards, wearing about
his feet what he should have placed upon his head,
making left of what is right, and so proceeding in
everything he does: there is only one good way to
bring him to account, and that is to make him do by
compulsion what he should have done through desire:
but the man of sense sees at once, what sooner or later,
must be, and does it to his joy, and to his credit.

❧ 2 6 9 ❧

C APITALIZE YOUR NOVELTY; for as long as
you are deemed new, you rate high. The novel
stands well everywhere because it is different; it
refreshes the taste, wherefore the brand-new mediocrity is more cherished than the shop-worn perfection.
The best of things grow grubby, and become old; only
note that this glory of the new is short-lived, and that
in four days respect for it will fade; know, therefore,
how to make use of these first days of approval, how to
catch this acclaim in its flight and seize all that is justly
yours; for when the fire of the new is spent, ardor

cools, and the excitement for the young will have to be exchanged for the boredom of the old; believe then that all that is yours also has its day, and that it passes.

270

D O NOT ALONE condemn what pleases the many. It must contain some good, to be so satisfying to the public, which even though it cannot be explained, must bring joy: the man who stands apart is always suspect, and when he is wrong, he becomes ridiculous; your action serves more to discredit your judgment, than the object, and so you are likely to be left alone in your bad taste; if you do not know how to strike upon the good, conceal your blindness; and do not condemn wholesale; for bad choice is ordinarily the child of ignorance: what all say, either is so, or is wished so.

271

L ET HIM WHO knows little, play safe, whatever his job, and even though he be not adjudged smart, he will be adjudged sound. He who knows much may take a chance, and let his imagination roam; but he who knows little, and takes chances, voluntarily tries suicide; hold always to the right, for what is established as right cannot be wrong; the king's highway is fixed for the simpleton, and this law for everybody, know he much, or know he little, there is better sense in safety, than in singularity.

ఇ **2 7 2** ఆ

SELL YOUR STUFF at the price of courtesy, for that imposes the heaviest obligation; never can the demand of a dealer raise the price to what is paid freely by the satisfied customer: courtesy not only pays, but it pledges, and it is gallant manner that imposes the greatest obligation; nothing costs a man of conscience more, than something given him, for it is sold him twice, and at a double price, that of its own value, and that of politeness. Nevertheless it remains true, that to men of mean spirit such noble talk is mere gibberish, for they do not understand the idioms of good style.

ఇ **2 7 3** ఆ

UNDERSTAND THE SPIRIT of those with whom you deal. In order to grasp their intent, for if the cause is well-understood, the effect is known; and from the first, the motive for the second. The melancholic perpetually augurs disaster, and the defamer, crime, in either instance the worst of what may be in the offing, for unable to encompass the existent good, each forecasts the possible evil: the man of passion always speaks of matters far differently from what they are, for he uses the terms of passion and not those of reason; thus does everyone babble according to his feelings or his mood, and all, very far from the truth; know how to read a face, and to decipher a soul from its lineaments; hold him who laughs ceaselessly as fool, and him who never laughs as false, on guard against the inquisitor, either because he is frivolous, or a spy; expect little good of men misborn, for they are given to revenging themselves upon nature, and as she showed little regard for them, they show little regard for her. Even so does a man tend to be the fool, as he is fair of face.

ᎧᏕ **2 7 4** ᎧᏕ

HAVE SOMETHING ATTRACTIVE about you, for its is the magic of civil intercourse; use this smooth hook more to catch goodwill, than good things, but always use it; merit is not enough, if it is not made to count through opportunity, for this is what brings forth acclaim; to have the cut, is to carry the best sceptre of rule, which even though most a matter of luck, can be helped by art, for where the ground is already rich, fertilization aids most; by such means popular yearning is created until all hearts are won.

ᎧᏕ **2 7 5** ᎧᏕ

JOIN IN, BUT not indecently. Not always the lead, and not always the clown, is to play the part of the gentleman, and some concession may be made to decorum to gain popularity; at times go as far as the crowd goes; but without becoming indecent: for he who is counted the fool in public will not be voted the sage in secret: more may be lost in one day of foolery than can be regained in a whole age of seriousness; but on this account do not forever stand apart; for to be thus singular is to condemn the others; much less act the prude, leaving this to its own sex, for even the too pious are ridiculous; the best a man can do is to appear the man, for a woman may play the man to perfection, but not the other way about.

৵ৼ **2 7 6** ৵ৼ

K NOW HOW TO refresh the spirit, through nature and through art; once in every seven years, so they say, we are made over, let it mark an elevation and realization of the better spirit: with the first seven years the intelligence enters, with each succeeding seven let some new virtue shine forth, and take note of this natural change in order to help it along, forever looking toward the improvement of all; of this it comes, that many have changed their deportment with change in social status or their business; which at times goes unnoticed, until the alteration has become excessive; at twenty, man is a peacock, at thirty a lion, at forty a camel, at fifty a snake, at sixty a dog, at seventy an ape, and at eighty, nothing.

༈ 2 7 7 ༀ

A MAN OF SHOW. Show is the spotlight for the talents. There is a moment for every one of them: seize it, for not every day will be its day of triumph. There be knights in armor of which even a little shines forth, and the much bedazzles. When now to their great gifts is added an ability to display them, these men pass as prodigies. There are nations that know how to put on, and it is Spain that does it superlatively. It was light that first revealed the whole of creation, and it is show that satisfies, supplying much and giving second life to everything, especially when joined to reality. The heavens from which springs every perfect thing, give to each its perfect setting, for either without the other would be sacrilege; only, exhibition requires art. Even that which is most excellent leans upon its surroundings, and every day is not its day. Show fares badly when out of season, for no attribute demands greater freedom from affectation, upon which it perishes, because so close to vanity, and this to cheapness: all ostentation must be much tempered, that it descend not to the vulgar, for by the understanding its excess is discredited. It reveals itself best perhaps in a silent eloquence, in a careless revelation of some high quality; wise concealment makes the most effective of parades, because such very secrecy most piques curiosity into life. A great trick not to exhibit all you have at once, but to allow frequent peeps, always bringing forward more. For one accomplishment must be the pledge of another and a greater, and the applause for the first, a welcome to those to follow.

ॐ **278** ॐ

AVOID ALL BADGES: for when they serve to mark you, even your distinctions become defects. All are the awards of peculiarity, which always raises question: for the singular is left to himself. Even beauty, when too surpassing, loses caste; whatever attracts notice, gives offence, especially in matters already of bad repute. But some seek prominence in vice itself, hunting for distinction in villainy, in order so to assure themselves an infamous notoriety. Even judgment, when too refined, degenerates into babble.

ॐ **279** ॐ

DO NOT ARGUE with an arguer. You must decide whether the argument springs from astuteness, or from asininity. It is not always pig-headedness but may be a trick. Pay heed, therefore, not to entangle yourself in the one, while disentangling yourself from the other. No precaution more in order, when with spies; and against the lockpickers of the soul, no better countertrick, than to leave the key of caution inside the door.

ঙ 2 8 0 ৯

A MAN OF PRINCIPLE. Right dealing is finished: truth is held the liar; good friends are few; for the best of service, the worst of pay; and this is the style the world over today. Whole nations are committed to evil dealings; with one you fear insecurity; with another, inconstancy, with a third, treason; wherefore, let this bad faith of others serve you, not as example, but as warning. The peril of the situation lies in the unhinging of your own integrity, at the sight of such baseness in conduct: but the man of principle never forgets what he is, because of what others are.

ঙ 2 8 1 ৯

THE GRACE OF those who understand. More to be cherished is the soft Yes of one man than the cheers of a whole crowd: because the belch of the froward, is not elevating: the sages speak with understanding, wherefore their praise brings lifelong satisfaction. Wise Antigonus reduced the whole theatre of his fame to one Zeno, and Plato called Aristotle his whole school. Some heed only to fill their stomachs, albeit with the worst of rubbish. Even the rulers need the grace of biographers, and they fear their pens more, than ugly women a painter's brush.

ఇక **2 8 2** ఇక

USE YOUR ABSENCE, to increase the respect and the honor in which you are held. If presence serves to diminish glory, absence serves to increase it. He who when absent was counted a lion, when present was counted ridiculous, and as something the mountain brought forth; the greatest gifts lose their lustre, when handled; for it is easier to see the husk than the rich interior of a spirit. The imagination goes far beyond what is glimpsed, and fraud, which commonly enters through the ears, has a way of going out through the eyes; he who keeps himself in the half-way place of public opinion regarding himself, keeps his reputation, for even the Phoenix makes capital of his absence in order to plume himself, and of the cry for him, in order to gain acclaim.

ఇక **2 8 3** ఇక

A MAN OF inventive mind. It marks the greatest genius, yet who can be such without a grain of dementia? Inventiveness springs from genius: good choice from the intelligence. The former is a gift from heaven, and most rare, but the capacity to choose right is given to many; the talent for discovery is vouch-safed to very few: and only to the first in their line, or in time. The new gives joy, and when of happy turn it puts a double halo upon the good. In matters of judgment it is dangerous, for seemingly paradoxical; but in matters of genius, it is laudable, and when either succeeds deserving of all praise.

❧ 2 8 4 ❧

BE NOT OBTRUSIVE, and so not slighted. Have respect for yourself, if you would be respected. Better pull than push. Arrive wanted, in order to arrive welcomed. Never to come without being invited, is to leave without being sent. He reaps all the indignation, who plows ahead on his own, if the thing goes badly; and none of the thanks if it goes well. The too froward is the lowest of the low, and because he pushes himself in with effrontery, he is pushed out in confusion.

❧ 2 8 5 ❧

DO NOT DIE of another's misery. Beware of him who is stuck in the mud, and note that he calls to you, to be comforted by your mutual unhappiness. These men are on the hunt for those who will help them carry their misfortune: and of those to whom in their prosperity they gave the cold shoulder, they today ask the hand. Great coolness is necessary with the drowning, if you would bring them help without peril to yourself.

ઃ 2 8 6 ઃ

NOT BEHOLDEN FOR everything, or to everybody, for that is to be a slave, and a common slave. Some are born luckier than others: the one that he may do more good, the other that he may receive it better. Independence is more precious, than any gift for which you might forfeit it. More satisfying far, that many depend upon you, than that you depend upon anybody. The power to command has only one advantage, the power to do greater good. But be most careful not to mistake an obligation put upon you for a favor, because usually the other's astuteness has so managed, that it will so appear.

ઃ 2 8 7 ઃ

DO NOTHING IN passion, or everything goes wrong. He cannot work for himself, who is not in command of himself and passion invariably banishes reason. Here have recourse to another more prudent, who may be anyone, provided unimpassioned. They who look on always see more, than those who are in the play, for they are not excited. As quickly as you discover yourself roused, let intelligence blow the retreat, for the blood has hardly rushed into the head, before all you do shows blood, and in one brief moment is spewed forth the substance of many days of shame for you, and of slander for another.

ಜ಼ **2 8 8** ಜ಼

LIVE AS CIRCUMSTANCE permits. All rule, all converse, everything must be determined by the contingency. Wish for what offers, for time and tide wait for no man. Do not journey through life by statute, even when such has the face of virtue, or indicate in terms too precise what alone will satisfy you, for tomorrow you may have to drink of the water that you disdained today. There are some so perverse, that they would have every circumstance of life fit itself to their vagaries and not the other way about: the man of wisdom knows better, and that the polar star of prudence is found by comporting himself according to the circumstance.

ಜ಼ **2 8 9** ಜ಼

THE GREATEST DEFECT in man, to give sign that he is a man, for he ceases to be held divine, from the day that he lets himself be seen human. Witlessness is the great head wind to renown. Just as the man discreet is held to be more than human; so the lightheaded is held to be less. There is no shortcoming, that cheapens more, for frivolousness stands directly opposed to earnestness. A fool can never prove himself a man of substance, especially if an old fool, when his years require that he have sense: and though this fault is the fault of many, it cannot be denied that it is peculiarly degrading.

ঙ্গ **2 9 0** ৵

A RARE JOY, to couple esteem with affection, but be not too much loved, if you would maintain the respect in which you are held: love is bolder than hatred: and affection and veneration, do not marry well; even though you may not be too much feared, you may not be too much loved, either. Affection ushers in familiarity, and for every step she takes forward, respect takes one backward. Better to be loved appreciatively than devotedly, for that is the love more befitting the great.

ঙ্গ **2 9 1** ৵

K NOW HOW TO analyze a man. The alertness of the examiner is matched against the reserve of the examined. But great judgment is called for, to take the measure of another. More important far to know the composition, and the properties of men, than those of herbs, and stones. This is the most delicate of the occupations of life: for the metals are known by their ring, and men by what they speak; words show forth the mind of a man; yet more, his works. To this end the greatest caution is necessary, the clearest observation, the subtlest understanding, and the most critical judgment.

﷼ **292** ﷼

WHAT YOU HAVE must exceed the requirements of your office, and not the other way about. For however high may be your post, you in your person must show yourself superior to it. A man of great qualifications, tends to grow, and to show this increasingly in his labors. But the man of mean heart, atrophies and soon reaches the end, both of his duties and his reputation. Great Augustus held himself greater as man, than as prince, to which end greatness of spirit avails much, and yet more an intelligent self-confidence.

﷼ **293** ﷼

BE MATURE. It gives radiance to the person, yet more to his personality, for as material weight makes precious the gold, moral weight, the man; it is the halo about every talent, and the reason for its veneration. The composure of a man is the façade of his spirit. This is not an old fool with the palsy, as silly humor would have it, but one with an authority most serene; he speaks with finality, and acts with certainty. It is the picture of the man complete; for each is held as much the man, as he has matured: and he began to be mature, and to carry authority, when he ceased to be a child.

❦ 2 9 4 ❧

B E MODERATE IN opinion. Every man believes as suits his interests: and he is filled with excuses for his stand. For, in most instances, judgment gives way to feeling. Thus two opinions confront each other and each believes that his is the side of reason: but she, always most fair, cannot be two-faced. The man of sense goes cautiously in so delicate a situation; and misgivings in his own mind moderate his judgment regarding that of another. At such moment let him imagine himself placed opposite: and examine therefrom the arguments, whereafter he will not utterly damn the other, nor yet justify himself entirely in what is so puzzling.

❦ 2 9 5 ❧

N OT A BLOWER, but a doer. They make the greatest show of what they have done, who have done least. Everything is made to appear marvelous and in the silliest fashion. Veritable chameleons for applause, they give everyone his fill of laughter. Conceit is always frowned upon, but here it is ridiculed. These ants of honor go collecting like beggars. But real achievement needs no such affectation. Rest in accomplishment, and leave talk to others. Do, and do not brag: nor with gold rent yourself a pen, for such writes dirt, that sickens the knowing. Aspire to be heroic, not only to seem it.

❧ 2 9 6 ❧

A MAN OF QUALITY, and of bearing. The first-rate makes the first-rate man, and one of these counts more than a thousand of the mediocre. There was he who was pleased that all he had was big, even to the kitchen-ware: how much more should the great man strive that the gifts of his spirit be such. Everything is infinite, everything immeasurable in God; and so must everything about a hero be great, and majestic; wherefrom it comes that all his acts, and even his thinking go clothed in one transcendent glory.

❧ 2 9 7 ❧

D EAL ALWAYS AS though seen. He is the seeing man, who sees that he is seen, or that he will be seen. He knows that the walls have ears, and that what is evil breaks its fetters to be free. Even when alone, he works as though the eyes of the world were upon him; because he knows that everything comes to be known; holding as witnesses today, those who will be such tomorrow because of what was discovered to them; unconcerned with what might be seen in his house from that of another, is only he who would have the whole world look in.

❧ 2 9 8 ❧

THREE THINGS MAKE the superman and they are the greatest gifts of divine generosity: a fertile mind, a deep understanding, and a cultivated taste. A great advantage, to have a good imagination; but a greater, to be able to think straight. To have a mind for what is good! Genius should not have its being in the spine, where it would be more steady, than ready. Straight thinking, is the fruit of reason. At twenty years desire rules us, at thirty, expediency, at forty, judgment. There are minds, that radiate light, like the eyes of the lynx, which in the greatest darkness see most clearly. Then there are those born for the occasion, who always strike upon what is most fitting: much awaits them, and a well-blessed harvest. But good taste lends flavor to all of life.

❧ 2 9 9 ❧

LEAVE HUNGER UNSATED: the cup must be torn from the lips even with its nectar. Desire is the measure of value, wherefore it is the trick of good taste, even for the thirst of the body, to satisfy, but not to sate; the good, when small, is doubly good. Great is the fall upon second appearance; and a surfeit of what is most pleasing, is dangerous, for it cheapens eternal quality itself. The only way to please your host, is to leave with an appetite still stimulated by a hunger still retained. If hurt must be felt, let it be that of a desire unsatisfied, rather than that of a satiety gratified; the happiness suffered for, is doubly sweet.

೫ 3 0 0 ೫

IN ONE WORD, a saint, for that is to say everything at once. For virtue is the bond of all the perfections, and the heart of all life's satisfactions. It makes a man sensible, alert, far-seeing, understanding, wise, courageous, considerate, upright, joyous, welcomed, truthful, and a universal idol. And three are the S's that make for happiness: saintliness, sanity and sapience. Virtue is the sun of our lesser world, the sky over which is a good conscience. It is so beautiful, that it finds favor of God, and of man. There is nothing lovely without virtue: and nothing hateful without vice: for virtue is the essence of wisdom, and all else is folly: capacity, and greatness must be measured in terms of virtue, and not in those of fortune. Virtue alone is sufficient unto itself: and it, only, makes a man worth loving in life, and in death, worth remembering.

❧ A f t e r w o r d ❧

An international book of knowledge has it that Baltasar Gracian appeared "toward the end of the 16th century." Calatayud is given as his birthplace, though Belmonte, a village near there, has become official. At eighteen Gracian became a member of the Society of Jesus and from that time on he was what we might call today a university man. The humanities, scripture, theology and philosophy are mentioned as the subjects of his teaching, and, for most of his life, the Jesuit College in Tarrogona was the place of his labors.

Seven volumes of his work were salvaged, edited and published by his Don Vincencio Juan de Lastanosa "without the permission of Gracian but not without his consent," as the commentators have it. Their titles are EL HEROE (THE MAN OF DISTINCTION), EL POLITICO DON FERNANDO EL CATOLICO (THE POLITIC FERNANDO), AGUDEZA Y ARTE DE INGENIO (WIT AND WAY), EL DISCRETO (THE MAN OF DISCERNMENT), and a three-volume work, EL CRITICON (THE MONITOR).

The ORACULO MANUAL Y ARTE DE PRUDENCIA that is here translated is not designated as the eighth of Gracian's volumes because it was created out of the rest. More, however, appears in the ORACULO than can be traced back to the enumerated works of the master. New paragraphs and new ideas evolve.

Credit for them must perhaps be given to Lastanosa who, while again appearing as Gracian's publisher, may well have been in this volume as in the earlier, much of a Boswell also. His address to the reader seems to prove this, for its brevity, its form and its total spirit are either tinctured by Gracian—or else much of Gracian must have been tinctured by him. In this paragraph Lastanosa counts the works of his friend as twelve; what became of the missing five is lost in the clouds of history. If, perchance, they existed as manuscripts, nothing is left of them now, for not even their titles, except in two instances, have come down to us.

Gracian failed to continue as rector of his Jesuit College, the chair of Scripture was taken from him, and he was ordered into the provinces. The Provost General wrote to the Provincial in Aragon: "Watch him, keep him in sight, at unexpected moments look into his cell and his papers and allow him nothing under lock and key therein." While in this state he died (December sixth, 1658) in the village of Tarazona in the province of Zaragoza, far from the place of his birth and still farther removed from the province of Tarragona and the place of his life's labor.

The estimates of Gracian as man or philosopher or writer run from the extremes of praise to the extremes of condemnation. His prose is the worst or the best in Spanish; his philosophy is commonplace or the renascence of pessimism; he was a shallow man of his times or an earnest student of the ways of getting heaven tied to earth. Himself, he praises the golden mean and that perhaps best characterizes him. The ORACULO is not food for babes and perhaps not philosophy for sages. But it is good spice—even though coca leaves may not be eaten for lettuce nor spirit be drunk raw.

Of the complete "works" of Gracian that have come down to us, the ORACULO MANUAL Y ARTE DE PRUDENCIA is that collection of three hundred paragraphs excerpted therefrom which his friend and editor Don Vincencio Juan de Lastanosa published for him. Issued late in the life of Gracian they represent the very heart of the man and, polished as they must have been by time and labor, the jewels of his soul. The ORACULO has been translated so often and into so many different languages that its reissue in English might seem to demand apology. And yet this is hardly so, for, frankly stated, all the translations (with the exception of Schopenhauer's into German) are so far removed from the Spanish original that simple justice to a man who was, would prove excuse enough for any new trial. Almost every translation of Gracian is but a translation from another translation—a matter carried to such ridiculous lengths that one of the German texts is translated from the Italian, itself translated from a French text which, corrupted in the extreme, derives from the Spanish; or else the translation comes out so distorted through the omissions, the emendations or the freightings of theological and scholastic bias that every semblance to the original picture is lost.

This translation is a straightforward attempt to express in English the thoughts of the ORACULO. I have made every effort to hold to the word, to that style of Gracian's which made famous a whole epoch of Spanish literature, and to the spirit of this thinker, thus attempting that impossible of the French wit who believes that translations are, like women, if true, rarely beautiful, and if beautiful, rarely true.

The apostrophes of Gracian are clipped, almost stenographic. They will not as such make appeal to a swift-reading public. But even by the slower-minded, the volume though small, cannot be read through at a sitting. And his words are barbed—at once to goad or to punish.

—*Martin Fischer*

ৰাষ Notes ৰাষ

❧ Notes ❧

❧ Notes ❧

❧ Notes ❧

❧ *Notes* ❧

ৰঙ Notes ৰঙ

Notes

Notes

Notes

Notes